THIS MAGICAL YEAR BELONGS TO:

# I Solemnly Swear
## That I'll Make the Most of this Magical Year

JANUARY

FEBRUARY

MARCH

APRIL

MAY

JUNE

Pull tarot cards, cast rune stones, or write your own
words of wisdom for each month of the year.

Fill them all out at the beginning of the
year, or do it month-by month as a "look
ahead" or a reflection of what's passed.

JULY

AUGUST

SEPTEMBER

OCTOBER

NOVEMBER

DECEMBER

Book Protection
Spell

Tuck sprigs of Mugwort,
Wormwood, or
St. John's Wort at both
the back and front
covers of the book.

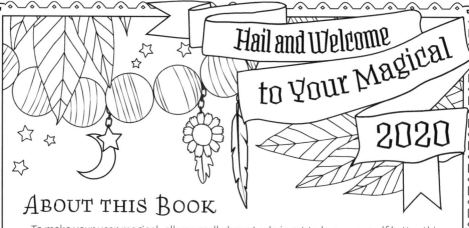

**Hail and Welcome to Your Magical 2020**

## ABOUT THIS BOOK

To make your year magical, all you really have to do is get to know yourself better this year than the year before. As a witch, you can claim control over your own destiny, harnessing intention, will, and natural forces already in play—such as the moon, the sun, and the changing seasons, also known as The Wheel of the Year.

You'll find the theme of "dark and light" several times in this book. The Wheel of the Year is a balance of dark and light. There is dark and light within each of our own selves. And there is a play of dark and light in art, shading, and coloring.

Doing witchcraft and art together is a powerful form of magic. Both of these practices call upon the same powers—the divine light within yourself—and the depths of the shadows that are behind it. Your own creative spirit is your magical power. Bringing art into your spiritual practice unlocks the magic of self expression—allowing you to see and feel a deeper understanding of who you are.

It takes courage to be yourself, to do art, to see what happens when you cast a spell. But as you take these steps to know yourself and to follow your soul's calling instead of living life to the expectations of others—you will find your own power.

You already have what you need to make the most of your magical life. All you have to do is start. And, most of all, be yourself... and have fun!

## HOW TO USE THIS PLANNER

There are no rules! It's all up to you. But here are some tips and suggestions:

• Don't stress about "keeping up" on coloring the whole book! You can color none of it, some of it, or all of it. Enjoy the parts you do, and don't worry if it doesn't all get "done."

• Since this book is printed on both sides of the paper, it works best if you use colored pencils, crayons, ballpoint pens, or gel pens. Markers will bleed through to the other side.

• Write, color, and draw in this book! Take notes. Expressing your thoughts in writing is a powerful way to create your reality. Here are some ideas of what to write: *Your day to day mundane appointments. Daily reflections. Daily tarot. A diary of your spiritual journey. Messages from your intuition. A daily gratitude journal.*

• The front of this book includes all sorts of things that you may find useful. It also has tips for using the astrological and moon phase information on the weekly calendar pages.

• "Spellcasting Basics" are included to show you how to cast a circle, ground and center, and perform a "full" spell. If you are new to spells, please be sure to read this.

• Always remember, the magic is inside you! Even if you start this book "late" in the year, or if it isn't "the best" moon phase, you are the most powerful force in your own life. The seasons, sun, and moon are only tools to help you unlock the magic you already have.

## Wield Thy Power... Witchy, Wonderful, Magical You!

## Goals, Plans, and Intentions

Yes, this is a planner, but that doesn't mean you have to get intense about... planning. It's about getting to know what you *really* want first and then using the powers of the universe to give you a boost. Work witchier, not harder! Here are some tips:

• Less is more. Go for broader feelings and intentions rather than super specific dates, processes, and outcomes. Leave room for magic to surprise you in fantastic ways.

• Make your goals as big or as small as you want. Your goal or plan could be to do less.

• Instead of saying what you don't want, "to stop being an emotional wreck," phrase it positively so you feel good when you say it, "to feel at ease with my emotions."

• Any plans you make are more of a guideline. Don't be afraid to scrap them and do something else if they don't feel right anymore. It's never too late to change directions or make new plans—in fact, that's often where the best magic comes in.

## Using Your Intuition

So how do you use your intuition? Follow your emotions. Emotions and intuition are woven of the same thread. Even if (especially if!) you've been called "too emotional," you can trust your emotions to be your guide. If something makes you feel "icky"— hurt, bad, anxious, nervous, hurried, chained, or dreary—stop and listen. Then figure out the message, work through it, let go of the unpleasant feelings, and restore your emotional balance by steering yourself to what feels better. Ask yourself, "Is this what I feel I *should* be doing, instead of what feels right for me?" And, "Is this what I want to do, or what someone else wants me to do?".

Can it really be that simple? Yes. It's the key to get you going in the right direction that only YOU can feel at any moment. So what is the direction to head for? The one that makes you feel happy, excited, hopeful, or curious. The one that feels better. Go that way.

## Dark, Light, and Shadow Selves

Following your good-feeling intuition doesn't mean you're "ignoring" your dark side. Just as the year has a dark half, we've all got a dark side or shadow selves—many of them. They are the unseen and often ignored parts of ourselves—self-doubt, low self-esteem, jealousy, fear, addiction, unhealthy habits, and stuckness. Whether you see shadows as obscuring the light or light as creating the shadows, this balance offers us the most powerful clues we have to our purpose and what we desire.

So... know that darkness. Use it. Acknowledge it. Know that both light and dark are essential halves of the magical seasons of your life, and the work is to walk through the shadows in order to transcend to a place of spiritual balance, purpose, and fulfillment. And, yes, this is a super-deep topic. There is so much more to explore here, so be sure to follow it if it calls you!

# Wheel of the Year

## Working with the Seasons & the Wheel of the Year

Think about ways you can work your life and magic in accordance with the Wheel of the Year and seasons. However, always choose what is right for you when it feels right, rather than waiting for "perfect" magical timing. Use these energies as a guideline, not as a rule. You can always start something new or let something go, no matter the season (or moon).

These cycles also remind us that there is a season of rest, reflection, and death on the opposite side of each season of growth, and that these dark times are essential parts of life.

---

*A Note About the Cross Quarter Dates: The dates for the two solstices and two equinoxes each year—Ostara, Litha, Mabon, and Yule—are calculated astronomically, from the position of the earth to the sun. The "cross quarter" festivals, which are the points between—Imbolc, Beltane, Lughnasadh, and Samhain—are often celebrated on "fixed" dates instead of the actual midpoints. And so, this book lists both the "Fixed Festival Dates" (above & listed on the calendars) where it's more common to celebrate, and the "Astronomical Dates" (listed on the calendars). Choose either date or any time in between for your own festivities or ritual. 'Tis the season for magic.

# The Seasons

# THE SUN IN THE ZODIAC

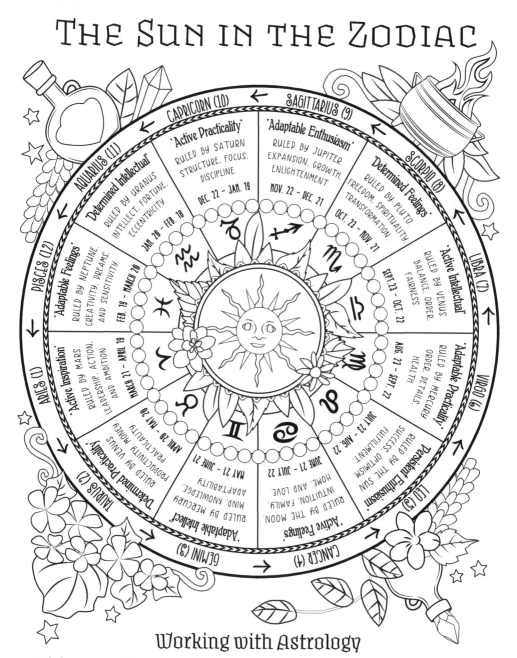

**CAPRICORN (10)**
"Active Practicality"
RULED BY SATURN.
STRUCTURE. FOCUS.
DISCIPLINE.
DEC. 22 – JAN. 19

**SAGITTARIUS (9)**
"Adaptable Enthusiasm"
RULED BY JUPITER.
EXPANSION. GROWTH.
ENLIGHTENMENT.
NOV. 22 – DEC. 21

**AQUARIUS (11)**
"Determined Intellectual"
RULED BY URANUS.
INTELLECT. FORTUNE.
ECCENTRICITY.
JAN. 20 – FEB. 18

**SCORPIO (8)**
"Determined Feelings"
RULED BY PLUTO.
FREEDOM. SPIRITUALITY.
TRANSFORMATION.
OCT. 23 – NOV. 21

**PISCES (12)**
"Adaptable Feelings"
RULED BY NEPTUNE.
CREATIVITY. DREAMS.
AND SENSITIVITY.
FEB. 19 – MARCH 20

**LIBRA (7)**
"Active Intellectual"
RULED BY VENUS.
BALANCE. ORDER.
FAIRNESS.
SEPT. 23 – OCT. 22

**ARIES (1)**
"Active Inspiration"
RULED BY MARS.
LEADERSHIP. ACTION.
AND AMBITION.
MARCH 21 – APRIL 19

**VIRGO (6)**
"Adaptable Practicality"
RULED BY MERCURY.
ORDER. DETAILS.
HEALTH.
AUG. 23 – SEPT. 22

**TAURUS (2)**
"Determined Practicality"
RULED BY VENUS.
PRODUCTIVITY. MONEY.
PRACTICALITY.
APRIL 20 – MAY 20

**LEO (5)**
"Persistent Enthusiasm"
RULED BY THE SUN.
SUCCESS. OPTIMISM.
FULFILLMENT.
JULY 23 – AUG. 22

**GEMINI (3)**
"Adaptable Intellect"
RULED BY MERCURY.
MIND. KNOWLEDGE.
ADAPTABILITY.
MAY 21 – JUNE 21

**CANCER (4)**
"Active Feelings"
RULED BY THE MOON.
INTUITION. FAMILY.
HOME. AND LOVE.
JUNE 21 – JULY 22

## Working with Astrology

Both the moon and the sun travel through the signs of the zodiac and can wield a powerful influence on our daily lives. These cycles are different from your "natal chart," and they affect the entire population as a whole.

The moon in the signs reflects what is going on subconsciously and emotionally. The sun in the signs represents a more conscious and outwardly noticeable influence. The sun stays in each sign for about a month. The moon's cycles are much shorter, just a couple of days at most.

It's also worth noting that this kind of astrology is "electional," meaning it's used to decide when to do things, as opposed to "predictive" astrology, where you might guess at future events.

To sync up with the energy of the moon and sun's cycles, look at the weekly calendar pages to note the current sign. Then, you can use that information and the charts on these pages to help you decide when to plan things and put the astrological energy more in your favor.

# The Moon in the Zodiac

## Aries ♈
A physical desire to start fresh. Energy for starting and completing short-term projects. Not the best time to start long-term projects.

## Taurus ♉
The sign of practical matters, the home, comfort, decor, and finances. An optimal moon sign for starting long-term projects.

## Gemini ♊
A time for thinking, learning, reading, pursuing curiosities and interests, doing mental activities, and talking to fascinating people.

## Cancer ♋
An auspicious time to be at home, reflect and get in touch with our feelings. Also an excellent time to focus on family and love.

## Leo ♌
The sign of the self and creativity. A magical time to get in touch with your own intuition and listen for what your heart truly desires.

## Virgo ♍
Organization, efficient habits, and health. The best time to start a routine or positive habit, organize, get on a schedule, or tidy things up.

## Libra ♎
The sign of diplomacy, balance, and visual appeal. A good time to work on relationships, find personal balance, and hang out with friends.

## Scorpio ♏
The sign of passion and desire. A good time to "find" motivation, harness your own power, take control, and rid yourself of things that no longer serve you.

## Sagittarius ♐
The sign of truth and big-picture visions. This is an auspicious time to make long-term plans, think big, use your imagination, and visualize a positive future.

## Capricorn ♑
The sign of structure, responsibilities, and practical achievement. A time to focus on career, business, and careful use of resources.

## Aquarius ♒
The sign of esoterica, freethinking, and personal freedom. A good time to expand your mind to find new, unexpected ideas and solutions.

## Pisces ♓
The sign of dreaming, psychic awareness, and intuition. An auspicious time for divination, reflection, mystical pursuits, and retreating into nature or water.

## Void-of-Course Moon

There are void-of-course spots in between the moon signs. These are the transitionary phases, and when the moon is void of course, there is a period of low energy where you may feel drained and exhausted or have trouble making decisions. Stores and businesses are "unusually" quiet, and people have trouble working together. It's also best not to start new projects or meet new people during the moon's void of course.

Often, you don't notice any difference because the void of course can be short—just a couple of minutes. But sometimes these periods can be hours or days, and that's when the shift in energy is quite noticeable! Being aware of these spots will help you use this energy to your advantage.

To see where these void spots are on the weekly calendar pages, look for the black triangles: ▶ These black triangles mark the start of the moon void-of-course cycle. The void ends when the moon enters the next sign.

# Planetary Retrogrades

Retrogrades happen when the planets appear to be moving backwards in our sky. When they're going backwards, they have the opposite effect as "normal," often causing confusion, blocks, or a need to "re-look" or "re-bel" or "re-treat" in their area of planetary influence. These occurrences are marked on the calendar pages, as it can be helpful to be aware of their possible influences and energies.

**MERCURY:** Mercury rules communication, so you may experience problems with technology, messages, or conversations when it is retrograde. Back up, double-check, and be extra careful with what you say and listen to. Prepare to be confused.

**VENUS:** Venus rules love and beauty, so be cautious about romantic relationships, exes, and changes in your physical appearance during Venus retrograde. Don't make a drastic change in your hair and appearance or sudden decisions with love.

**MARS:** Mars rules power and success, so don't start something big and new when Mars is retrograde. Make sure to think through career or business decisions. You may feel particularly slow or unenergized.

**JUPITER:** Jupiter rules travel, expansion, higher education, and finances, so you may have issues with transportation or trouble making progress when trying to expand or grow your business or career during Jupiter retrograde. It's a good time to slow down, make sure not to overspend, and to take time to learn, study, and experiment.

**SATURN:** Saturn rules responsibility, structure, and discipline, and is often an illuminator of limitations. So when it goes retrograde, it gives an opportunity to move past failure and see beyond boundaries and comfort zones.

**NEPTUNE:** Neptune rules illusion, dreams, spirituality, and fantasy, so as these influences disappear during a retrograde, you may feel the stark reality of things you normally do not see. Use this time to relook at the truth versus what you've been telling yourself and find clues on how to bring dreams to reality.

**URANUS:** Uranus rules the unexpected, things involving change, liberation, and innovation. Uranus retrograde can push you to big realizations, where you can see past your limitations and fears. This retrograde can show you where you need to make changes.

**PLUTO:** Pluto rules the shadow and the underworld. During a Pluto retrograde, look at your shadow self and your needs for recognition, authority, and power. It's a good time to discover your shadow and find ways to work through the darkness.

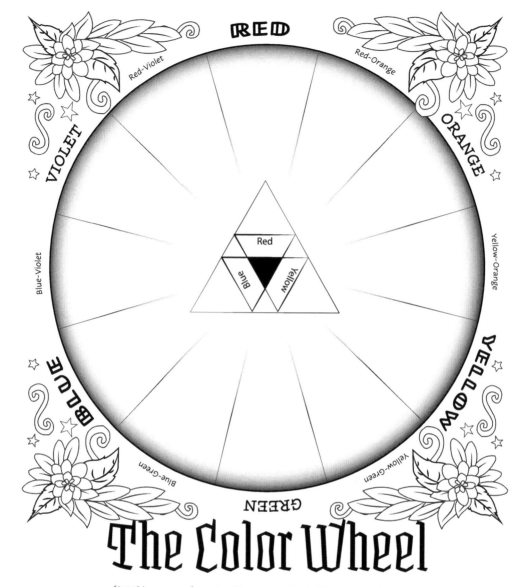

# The Color Wheel

*(Get this page as a free printable at coloringbookofshadows.com/colorwheel)*

Color is science and magic. The color wheel shows what happens when you mix the primary colors of red, yellow, and blue. You get a rainbow, which is pure awesomeness.

The secondary colors are what's in-between the primaries—orange, green, and violet (purple). And the steps between those are called tertiary colors, shown above in the smallest font.

There are two approaches to color this wheel:

1. The scientific way (which might not look as tidy) is a real-life experiment. Use only three primary pencil colors, red, yellow, and blue, and blend and overlap them to mix all of the other colors in-between. This will show you how color "works."

2. Or you can color it in a way that's more true to the eye and to test out your pencils. Use twelve pencils, all of the colors shown above (or just use six pencils, primary and secondary, and blend in the tertiary!).

Once you've picked a method, start blending the colors into each other. Try to blend as dark as you can towards the outside of the wheel, and fade it out as light as you can go, to white, at the center. A black outer edge is started for you above, but feel free to deepen this dark edge by blending further with a black pencil!

This will demonstrate how each color looks when it's mixed with black (a shade!) and with white (a tint!).

# Where's Brown?!

Did you notice that the previous color wheel doesn't include any gorgeous earthy browns?!

That's because brown is on the secondary color wheel, which blends the three secondary colors of orange, green, and violet. You can find brown hidden between violet (purple) and orange. Go ahead and try! Amazing, yes?

Filling out this secondary color wheel will also show you how you can use three really "bright" colors like green, orange, and purple—but keep it more neutral by using browns... and the other colors hidden in between!

*Inspired by the Moses Harris Color Wheels, 1776*

# Choosing Color Combinations

It's definitely okay to pick your colors by heart or by feel or by spirit or with your eyes closed or however you want. Go for it!

But if you're intrigued to know more about color, you can use color schemes to get some cool results, both visually and magically.

COMPLEMENTARY is two opposites on the color wheel. This can be used to balance and contrast two things in your magic or coloring.

MONOCHROMATIC uses the same shades and tints of just one color. You can give this scheme contrast by using tints and shades.

ANALOGOUS usually uses three or more colors in a row, such as all of the colors from orange to green, or orange to yellow.

SPLIT COMPLEMENTARY uses three colors in the shape of a witch's hat. Pick a color, find its complementary color, then "split" that by using the colors to the left and right, such as violet, yellow-green, and yellow-orange.

TRIADIC uses three colors that form an equilateral triangle. The primary triad uses red, yellow, and blue, for example.

TETRADIC is made of four colors that form a square or rectangle on the color wheel, such as violet, red, green, and yellow.

| COMPLEMENTARY | MONOCHROMATIC | ANALOGOUS | SPLIT-COMPLEMENTARY | TRIADIC | TETRADIC |

So you've picked your colors from the color wheel.... now what? Well, this is just a starting point! You could do a mostly monochromatic color scheme with a few accents that are split-complementary, or an analogous color scheme with complimentary accents. Or you might use lots of neutrals and add some contrasting tetradic colors! Try a few:

Try your hand at using two
**COMPLEMENTARY COLORS**

What if you use just one
**MONOCHROMATIC COLOR?**

Practice shading this with three
**ANALOGOUS COLORS + BROWN**

Try this one with BEIGE + three
**SPLIT-COMPLEMENTARY COLORS**

Shade with GREY + three
**TRIADIC COLORS**

And see what you can do with four
**TETRADIC COLORS**

# Light & Shadow

*No pressure here! Feel free to skip this section and color any way you like, or not at all.*

But if you're looking to add depth and some interesting effects to your coloring—try working with light and shadow. The awesome thing about using "light and shadow" in art is that it mirrors how their dynamic works spiritually. There is always dark or shadow opposite of the light. Ta-dah! And you can work with this power and balance in crayon and within yourself.

Try looking at the white of the page as a light. Really visualize it! Where is it coming from? How bright is it? Then start to add color and shading to fill in the density and shadow of the objects as they fall on the page and as they obscure the light. Keep visualizing and shading to get the depth of shadow and "dark" that you desire in contrast.

## WHERE IS YOUR LIGHT?!

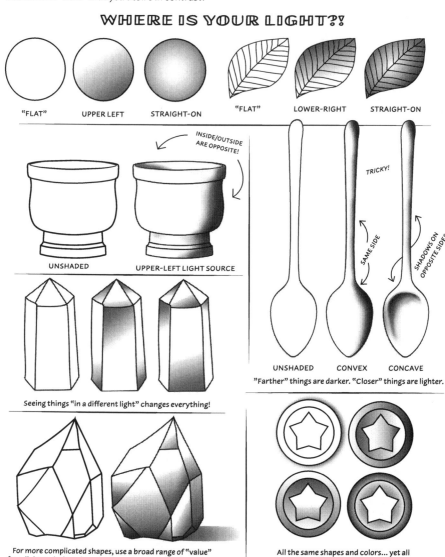

"FLAT"    UPPER LEFT    STRAIGHT-ON

"FLAT"    LOWER-RIGHT    STRAIGHT-ON

INSIDE/OUTSIDE ARE OPPOSITE!

UNSHADED    UPPER-LEFT LIGHT SOURCE

TRICKY!

SAME SIDE

SHADOWS ON OPPOSITE SIDES

UNSHADED    CONVEX    CONCAVE

"Farther" things are darker. "Closer" things are lighter.

Seeing things "in a different light" changes everything!

For more complicated shapes, use a broad range of "value" from light to dark to show depth, contrast, and luminescence.

All the same shapes and colors... yet all are wildly different in light and shadow!

# Color Magic

 **WHITE**
Peace & light

 **RED**
Power & Passion

 **GREEN**
Abundance & Spirit

 **BLACK**
Mystery & Shadow

 **ORANGE**
Courage

 **BLUE**
Calm & Awareness

 **BROWN**
Earth & Belonging

**YELLOW**
Happiness & Joy

 **PURPLE**
Spirituality

Colors are also known for their magical and energetic properties. You often hear about colors in candle magic, but color can be used in all kinds of spells. "Color magic" means working with the energies of the color's vibrations to attract or repel things.

You can reference correspondence sheets to get started (like the very basic one above), but working with color is a personal experience. Everyone sees and feels colors differently. Focus on how colors make you feel and pick the ones that call to you, even if you're using the color wheel for guidance.

The shades and tints within each color can have contrasting feelings. There are shades of blue that feel empty and ominous and others that are calm and peaceful. If it emotes a feeling within you, it has power. Use this power in your art and spellwork!

## HOW TO BANISH CREATIVE BLOCKS & FEARS

It's your spirit—not your skill—that'll make your coloring turn out wonderfully. Sure, you may develop skills, but they are an added bonus, and not the journey or the magic.

The two most common and totally brutal, soul-crushing "creative blocks" are:

1. Comparison. Judging your skills and outcome based on anyone else's art will kill your creativity. It'll suck all of the fun and life out in one dreadful jab from your shadow-self.

2. Thinking about what other people will think about your art (good or bad!). This is an excellent way to ruin the experience and spirit of the occasion.

Well, how do you banish these creativity slayers? You triumph with the brightness of your own light, and by allowing the art to become a channel for spirit to flow through you.

*A little creativity spell:* Pick up a pencil. Then imagine a column of light of many colors—the creative spirit or your divine self—coming in through the top of your head. Feel the light going down your neck, through your shoulders, slowly rolling down your arms, and into your hands, and through your pencil. Then, start coloring.

And let the mystery unfold! You'll never know how your art or coloring is going to turn out when you start, so let go of that right away. Sure, you can visualize how you want it to look and try for a certain vibe—but then let your spirit breathe life into it. Trust in yourself as the magic (and gorgeous art!) is revealed from within you.

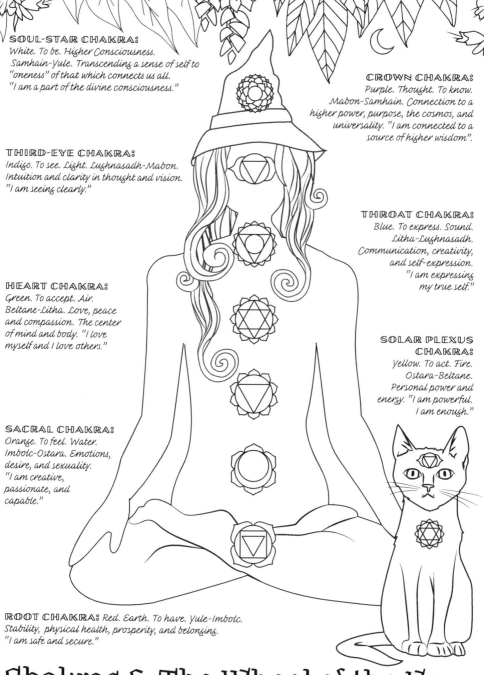

**SOUL-STAR CHAKRA:**
*White. To be. Higher Consciousness.*
*Samhain-Yule. Transcending a sense of self to*
*"oneness" of that which connects us all.*
*"I am a part of the divine consciousness."*

**CROWN CHAKRA:**
*Purple. Thought. To know.*
*Mabon-Samhain. Connection to a*
*higher power, purpose, the cosmos, and*
*universality. "I am connected to a*
*source of higher wisdom".*

**THIRD-EYE CHAKRA:**
*Indigo. To see. Light. Lughnasadh-Mabon.*
*Intuition and clarity in thought and vision.*
*"I am seeing clearly."*

**THROAT CHAKRA:**
*Blue. To express. Sound.*
*Litha-Lughnasadh.*
*Communication, creativity,*
*and self-expression.*
*"I am expressing*
*my true self."*

**HEART CHAKRA:**
*Green. To accept. Air.*
*Beltane-Litha. Love, peace*
*and compassion. The center*
*of mind and body. "I love*
*myself and I love others."*

**SOLAR PLEXUS**
**CHAKRA:**
*Yellow. To act. Fire.*
*Ostara-Beltane.*
*Personal power and*
*energy. "I am powerful.*
*I am enough."*

**SACRAL CHAKRA:**
*Orange. To feel. Water.*
*Imbolc-Ostara. Emotions,*
*desire, and sexuality.*
*"I am creative,*
*passionate, and*
*capable."*

**ROOT CHAKRA:** *Red. Earth. To have. Yule-Imbolc.*
*Stability, physical health, prosperity, and belonging.*
*"I am safe and secure."*

# Chakras & The Wheel of the Year

Chakra means "wheel" or "disc." Chakras are energy centers within you that spin, generate, and move prana or life-force energy.

The concept of chakras is thousands of years old. There is a wondrous depth of wisdom written on the subject, if it calls you for further study.

Each of the chakras corresponds to a color in ancient Vedic practice, and by interweaving traditions, the chakras can cross-correspond to the spokes on the Celtic Wheel of the Year.

Try using these time frames over your year to focus on working with each chakra.

# Scrying & Divination Basics

"Elemental Scrying" is the practice of looking for intuitive guidance and wisdom within nature. It is a form of divination, which isn't a future-telling practice, but a way of seeing the energies and things that already are within you, around you, and influencing you.

The four seasons can correspond to one of the four elements (the fifth element is spirit or self—your own inner guidance and being), and elemental scrying can feel even more powerful when practiced in the corresponding season.

Ideas for scrying can be found within this book, in March (Air, Spring), June (Fire, Summer), September (Water, Autumn), and December (Earth, Winter). However, feel free to use any of these methods anytime during the year.

In scrying, you typically have to "see" the symbolism yourself—nothing is drawn out for you systematically like in tarot or runes. And so, scrying works best with patience and a vivid imagination.

Clear your mind, then "gaze" your eyes to let go of your focus. Look for shapes, letters, numbers, and patterns in your scrying tool but also sense for feelings and sudden thoughts. The message could be visual, something you see, or auditory, something you hear—either in your mind or in nature, like a bird—or it could be a feeling that comes over you suddenly. It could be a message in the physical world, something that someone says, or it could be in your mind or internal being, a feeling, sense, or vision.

With any method of divination, you may not "get" the message right away. Write down any attempts you make to scry or divine and any results, whether it's accidental, purposeful, or nonsensical.

Take notice of clues, coincidences, and patterns that present themselves during or after your scrying session. They are not random. You are noticing them for a reason. You might catch a glimpse of something in a reflective surface or see a coincidental shape in the clouds that resonates with you. This, too, is scrying. It doesn't only count when you are "trying" to see a message or find an answer.

# Spellcasting Basics

There are opening and closing steps that are basic accompaniments to spells in this book. These steps are optional but advisable: at least know "why" many witches perform these processes and try them out for yourself.

And keep in mind, this is a super basic "coloring book" guide to the spellcasting process. There are books and online sources that go much further in-depth.

### THE SECRET OF SPELLS

The secret to powerful spells is in you. Your feeling and vibration in alignment with your true source of self—or a higher power—is what makes spells work.

The secret isn't in having the right ingredients and doing all the steps in a particular order. It's in your ability to focus your intent and use your feelings, mind, and soul to call in what you want and harness the energy of the earth, plants, stars, moons, planets, and whatever other creative forces of life you like to make things happen.

### BREAK THE RULES

The first rule is to throw out any of the rules that don't work for you. Do things that feel right, significant, and meaningful. Adapt spells from different practices, books, and teachers. The only way to know what works is to follow your curiosity and try things out.

### USING TOOLS

Your feelings and vibration are what make the magic, not the tools, exact words, or sequences. You can cast amazing spells for free with no tools at all, and you can cast an elaborate spell that yields no results.

That said, tools like herbs, oils, crystals, and cauldrons can be powerful and fun to use in your spells. Just don't feel pressured or discouraged if you don't have much to start. Keep your magic straightforward and powerful. The right tools and ingredients will come.

### "AS ABOVE, SO BELOW"

Tools, ingredients, and symbols are based on the magical theory of sympathetic magic and correspondence. You might hear the phrase, "As Above, So Below," which means the spiritual qualities of objects are passed down to earth. It's "sympathetic magic," or "this equals that," like how a figure of a lion represents that power but is not an actual lion.

Start by following lists, charts, and spells to get a feel for what others use and then begin to discover your own meaningful symbolism and correspondences.

PERMISSION

Spellbooks are like guidelines. They should be modified, simplified, or embellished to your liking. And don't degrade your magic by calling it "lazy." Keeping your witchcraft simple is okay. Go ahead, you have permission.

Also, it's not a competition to see who can use the most esoteric stuff in their spell. Hooray! It's about finding your personal power and style.

SPELLCASTING OUTLINE:

1. Plan and prepare.
2. Cast a circle.
3. Ground and center.
4. Invoke a deity or connection to self.
4. Raise energy.
5. Do your spellcraft (like the spells in this book).
6. Ground and center again.
7. Close your circle.
8. Clean up.
9. Act in accord (and be patient!).

**1. PLAN AND PREPARE:** If you're doing a written spell, read it several times to get familiar with it. Decide if there's anything you'll substitute or change. If you're writing your own spell, enjoy the process and mystery of seeing the messages and theme come together.

Gather all of the items you'll be using (if any) and plan out space and time where you'll do the spell. Spells can be impromptu, so preparations can be quick and casual if you like.

**2. CAST A CIRCLE AND CALL THE QUARTERS:** A circle is a container to collect the energy of your spell. Circles are also protective, with the circle of white light elevating your space and spell to the highest vibration and clearing out any negativity that might get in the way before you begin. Calling the Quarters is done to get the universal energy of the elements flowing. Incense is typically burned at the same time to purify the air and energy. If you can't burn things, that's ok. If you've never cast a circle, try it. It's a fun, mystical experience like no other. Once you have a few candles lit and start to walk around it, magic does happen!

**HOW TO CAST A CIRCLE:** This is a basic, bare-bones way to cast a circle. It's often much more elaborate, and this explanation barely does it justice, so read up to find out more. And note that while some cast the circle first and then call the Quarters, some do it the other way around.

1. Hold out your hand, wand, or crystal, and imagine a white light and a sphere of pure energy surrounding your space, as you circle around clockwise three times. Your circle can be large or it can be tiny, just space for you and your materials.

2. Call The Four Quarters or Five Points of the Pentagram, depending on your preferences. The Quarters (also known as the Elements!) are Earth (North), Air (East), Fire (South), and Water (West). Many use the Pentagram and also call the 5th Element, Spirit or Self.

Face in each direction and say a few words to welcome the element. For example, "To the North, I call upon your power of grounding and strength. To the East, I call upon the source of knowledge. To the South, I call upon your passion and burning desire to take action. To the West, I call upon the intuition of emotion. To the Spirit and Source of Self, I call upon your guidance and light."

**3. GROUND AND CENTER:** Grounding and centering prepare you to use the energy from the earth, elements, and universe. Most witches agree that if you skip these steps, you'll be drawing off of your own energy, which can be exhausting and ineffective. It's wise to ground and center both before and after a spell. It's like the difference between being "plugged into" the magical energy of the earth and universe and "draining your batteries."

How to Ground and Center: To ground, imagine the energy coming up from the core of the earth and into your feet, as you breathe deeply. You can visualize deep roots from your feet all the way into the center of the earth, with these roots drawing the earth's energy in and out of you. The point is to allow these great channels of energy to flow through you and into your spell. You can also imagine any of your negative energy, thoughts, or stress leaving.

To center, once you've got a good flow of energy from the ground, imagine the energy shining through and out the top of your head as a pure form of your highest creative self and then back in as the light of guidance. Suspend yourself here between the earth and the sky, supported with the energy flowing freely through you, upheld, balanced, cleansed, and "in flow" with the energy of the universe. This process takes just a couple of minutes.

**4. RAISE ENERGY:** The point of raising energy is to channel the universal (magical!) forces you tapped into through the previous steps to use in your spell. And raising energy is fun! You can sing, dance, chant, meditate, or do breath work. You want to do something that feels natural, so you can really get into it, lose yourself, and raise your state of consciousness.

A good way to start is to chant "Ong," allowing the roof of your mouth to vibrate ever so slightly. This vibration changes up the energy in your mind, body, and breath and is a simple yet powerful technique.

Another tip is to raise energy to the point of the "peak" where you feel it at its highest. Don't go too far where you start to tucker out or lose enthusiasm!

**INVOKE A DEITY OR CREATIVE SOURCE:** If you'd like to invoke a deity or your highest self to help raise energy and your

vibration, call upon them. Invoking deities is way deeper than this book, so research it more if it calls to you!

**5. DO YOUR SPELL:** Your spell can be as simple as saying an intention and focusing on achieving the outcome of what you want, or it can be more elaborate. Whichever way you prefer, do what feels right to you.

**TIPS ON VISUALIZATION AND INTENTION**

Most spellwork involves a bit of visualization and intention, and here are some subtleties you can explore.

**The Power of You:** The most important tool in magic is you. You've got it—both power right now and vast untapped power that you can explore. To cast a successful spell, you've got to focus your mind and genuinely feel the emotions and feelings of the things you want to manifest.

If you haven't started meditating yet, start now! It's not too late, and it's easier than you think.

**Visualize the Outcome**

It's best to focus on the feeling of what you want, not the process of getting there. Feel the completion of your desire, and feel it powerfully.

For example, you could repeat the mantra "I have all the money I need" while feeling uneasy and worried about money in your spell, but this probably won't work. You've got to visualize and really feel the sense of calm and control you'll have when you do get the desired outcome, be it money or whatever else.

**Phrase it Positively**

Another tip is to phrase your intentions and desires positively. You're putting energy into this, so make sure the intention is going to be good for you. Instead of saying what you don't want, "to get out of my bad job that I hate," phrase it positively, "I want to do something that's fulfilling with my career." Then you'll be able to feel good about it, as you visualize and cast your spell.

## 6. GROUND AND CENTER AGAIN

After your spell, it's important to ground out any excess energy. Do this again by visualizing energy flowing through you and out. You can also imagine any "extra" energy you have petering out as you release it back into the earth.

## 7. CLOSE YOUR CIRCLE

If you called the Quarters or a deity, let them know the spell has ended by calling them out again.

Close your circle the opposite of as you opened it, circling around three times or more counterclockwise. Then say, "This circle is closed," or do a closing chant or song to finish your spell.

## 8. CLEAN UP

Don't be messy with your magic! Put away all of your spell items.

**9. ACT IN ACCORD:** Once you cast your spell, you've got to take action! You can cast a spell that you become a best-selling author, but if you never write a book, it's never going to happen. So you've got to take action towards what you want to open up the possibility and opportunity for it to come to you.

Look for signs, intuition, and coincidences that point you in the direction of your desires. If you get inspired after a spell, take action! Don't be surprised if you ask for money and then come up with a new idea to make money.

Follow those clues, especially if they feel exciting and good.

If your spell comes true, discard and "release" any charm bag, poppet, or item you used to hold and amplify energy. Also, give thanks (if that's in your practice) or repay the universe in some way, doing something kind or of service that you feel is a solid trade for what you received from your spell.

## WHAT IF YOUR SPELL DOESN'T WORK?

It's true that not all spells will work! But sometimes the results are just taking longer than you'd like, so be patient.

If your spell doesn't work, you can use divination or meditation to do some digging into reasons why.

The good news is your own magic, power, frequency, and intention is still on your side. You can try again and add more energy in the direction of your desired outcome by casting another spell.

Give it some deep thought. What else is at play? Did you really take inspired action? Are you totally honest with yourself about what you want? Are there any thoughts or feelings about your spell that feel "off"? Are you grateful for what you already have? Can you "give back" or reciprocate with service or energy?

## FOR MORE TIPS AND INSPIRATION:

Seek out websites, books, podcasts, and videos on spirituality. Follow your intuition and curiosity to deepen your practice and find your own style. And check out other books in the *Coloring Book of Shadows* series, like the *Book of Spells* and *Witch* Life!

# 1ST HALF 2020

## January

| S | M | T | W | Th | F | Sa |
|---|---|---|---|---|---|---|
|  |  |  | 1 | ◑ | 3 | 4 |
| 5 | 6 | 7 | 8 | 9 | ○ | 11 |
| 12 | 13 | 14 | 15 | 16 | ◐ | 18 |
| 19 | 20 | 21 | 22 | 23 | ● | 25 |
| 26 | 27 | 28 | 29 | 30 | 31 |  |

## February

| S | M | T | W | Th | F | Sa |
|---|---|---|---|---|---|---|
|  |  |  |  |  |  | ◑ |
| 2 | 3 | 4 | 5 | 6 | 7 | 8 |
| ○ | 10 | 11 | 12 | 13 | 14 | ◑ |
| 16 | 17 | 18 | 19 | 20 | 21 | 22 |
| ● | 24 | 25 | 26 | 27 | 28 | 29 |

## March

| S | M | T | W | Th | F | Sa |
|---|---|---|---|---|---|---|
| 1 | ◑ | 3 | 4 | 5 | 6 | 7 |
| 8 | ○ | 10 | 11 | 12 | 13 | 14 |
| 15 | ◐ | 17 | 18 | 19 | 20 | 21 |
| 22 | 23 | ● | 25 | 26 | 27 | 28 |
| 29 | 30 | 31 |  |  |  |  |

## April

| S | M | T | W | Th | F | Sa |
|---|---|---|---|---|---|---|
|  |  |  | ◑ | 2 | 3 | 4 |
| 5 | 6 | ○ | 8 | 9 | 10 | 11 |
| 12 | 13 | ◑ | 15 | 16 | 17 | 18 |
| 19 | 20 | 21 | ● | 23 | 24 | 25 |
| 26 | 27 | 28 | 29 | ◑ |  |  |

## May

| S | M | T | W | Th | F | Sa |
|---|---|---|---|---|---|---|
|  |  |  |  |  | 1 | 2 |
| 3 | 4 | 5 | 6 | ○ | 8 | 9 |
| 10 | 11 | 12 | 13 | ◐ | 15 | 16 |
| 17 | 18 | 19 | 20 | 21 | ● | 23 |
| 24 | 25 | 26 | 27 | 28 | ◑ | 30 |
| 31 |  |  |  |  |  |  |

## June

| S | M | T | W | Th | F | Sa |
|---|---|---|---|---|---|---|
|  | 1 | 2 | 3 | 4 | ○ | 6 |
| 7 | 8 | 9 | 10 | 11 | 12 | ◑ |
| 14 | 15 | 16 | 17 | 18 | 19 | 20 |
| ● | 22 | 23 | 24 | 25 | 26 | 27 |
| ◑ | 29 | 30 |  |  |  |  |

# 2ND HALF 2020

## July

| S | M | T | W | Th | F | Sa |
|---|---|---|---|---|---|---|
|  |  |  | 1 | 2 | 3 | 4 |
|  | 6 | 7 | 8 | 9 | 10 | 11 |
|  | 13 | 14 | 15 | 16 | 17 | 18 |
| 19 | 20 | 21 | 22 | 23 | 24 | 25 |
| 26 | 27 | 28 | 29 | 30 | 31 |  |

## August

| S | M | T | W | Th | F | Sa |
|---|---|---|---|---|---|---|
|  |  |  |  |  |  | 1 |
| 2 | 3 | 4 | 5 | 6 | 7 | 8 |
| 9 | 10 | 11 | 12 | 13 | 14 | 15 |
| 16 | 17 | 18 | 19 | 20 | 21 | 22 |
| 23 | 24 | 25 | 26 | 27 | 28 | 29 |
| 30 | 31 |  |  |  |  |  |

## September

| S | M | T | W | Th | F | Sa |
|---|---|---|---|---|---|---|
|  |  | 1 | 2 | 3 | 4 | 5 |
| 6 | 7 | 8 | 9 | 10 | 11 | 12 |
| 13 | 14 | 15 | 16 | 17 | 18 | 19 |
| 20 | 21 | 22 | 23 | 24 | 25 | 26 |
| 27 | 28 | 29 | 30 |  |  |  |

## October

| S | M | T | W | Th | F | Sa |
|---|---|---|---|---|---|---|
|  |  |  |  | 1 | 2 | 3 |
| 4 | 5 | 6 | 7 | 8 | 9 | 10 |
| 11 | 12 | 13 | 14 | 15 | 16 | 17 |
| 18 | 19 | 20 | 21 | 22 | 23 | 24 |
| 25 | 26 | 27 | 28 | 29 | 30 | 31 |

## November

| S | M | T | W | Th | F | Sa |
|---|---|---|---|---|---|---|
| 1 | 2 | 3 | 4 | 5 | 6 | 7 |
| 8 | 9 | 10 | 11 | 12 | 13 | 14 |
| 15 | 16 | 17 | 18 | 19 | 20 | 21 |
| 22 | 23 | 24 | 25 | 26 | 27 | 28 |
| 29 | 30 |  |  |  |  |  |

## December

| S | M | T | W | Th | F | Sa |
|---|---|---|---|---|---|---|
|  |  | 1 | 2 | 3 | 4 | 5 |
| 6 | 7 | 8 | 9 | 10 | 11 | 12 |
| 13 | 14 | 15 | 16 | 17 | 18 | 19 |
| 20 | 21 | 22 | 23 | 24 | 25 | 26 |
| 27 | 28 | 29 | 30 | 31 |  |  |

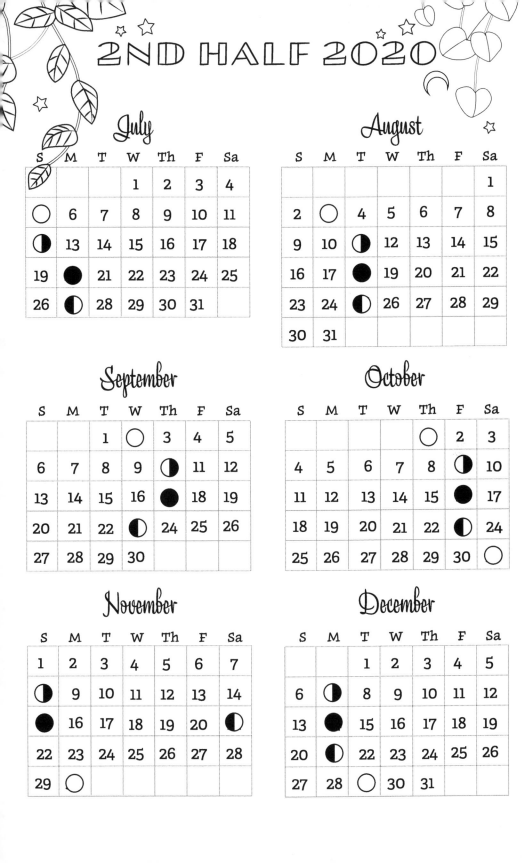

INTUITION:

REFLECTION:

VISION & INTENTION:

IMPORTANT THINGS:

La Befana
Renewal of Spirit

GOALS:

Affirmation:
I am safe and secure.
I know and trust myself.

Currants - Fennel - Anise - Citrus - Brandy

# January

Wolf - Inner Wisdom

Rosemary & Wintergreen - Protection & Purification

Red Jasper - Grounding & Nurturing

# Wolf Moon

## MOON ENERGY AND SPELL IDEAS

NEW & WAXING MOON: Grounding, healing, and gaining knowledge about your true self.
FULL MOON: Self-acceptance, belonging, and belief in yourself and your power.
WANING & DARK MOON: Letting go of insecurities. Banishing ill health and bad luck.

Raven - Transformation

Carnation - Strength & Fresh Energy

Thread - Weaving Your Future

Owl - Magic & Vision

SO SHALL IT BE

# ANIMAL STITCH WITCHERY
## CRAFTING TO CONNECT TO YOUR INNER POWER

The depths of the winter present the opportunity to retreat and recharge.

Animal guides evoke a primal sense of belonging, and from this place, you can connect to your own innate being and true self.

In this spell, you'll use the magic of creativity and craft to channel an animal guide.

Things You'll Need: Find your animal guide... or let it find you. You might already know an animal guide, but if not, find one in whatever way suits your magical practice. Get to know the symbolism and wisdom of the animal, as well as the way it moves, acts, and lives in the wild.

Prepare supplies for a craft project that depicts your animal guide. Embroidery! Cross-stitch! Clay! Crochet! A figurine or photo will work if you don't want to craft something.

Cast the Spell: With your craft supplies gathered 'round, light incense that awakens your creative spirit or embodies your animal's habitat, such as citrus, pine, eucalyptus, or cedar.

Ask to channel the power and wisdom of the animal. As you craft, you can allow yourself silence or repeat a mantra. Anything empowering (or silent!) will do. For example:

*The spirit's in me. A branch of the tree.*
*I am the (animal). And so I shall be.*

When finished, place your animal craft in a location of reverence, such as your altar. Use your animal charm in spells or rituals, or anytime you want to ground and re-energize your spirit and inner strength.

# January 2020

| | SUNDAY | MONDAY | TUESDAY |
|---|---|---|---|
| | 29 | 30 | 31 |
| | 5 | 6 | 7 |
| | 12 | 13 | 14 |
| | 19 | 20 | 21 |
| | 26 | 27 | 28 |

| WEDNESDAY | THURSDAY | FRIDAY | SATURDAY |
|---|---|---|---|
| 1 | 2 ◑ First Quarter | 3 | 4 |
| 8 | 9 | 10 ○ Full Moon | 11 |
| 15 | 16 | 17 ◐ Last Quarter | 18 |
| 22 | 23 | 24 ● New Moon | 25 |
| 29 | 30 | 31 | 1 ◑ First Quarter |

# January 2020

## MONDAY, DECEMBER 30, 2019
▶ Moon void-of-course begins 5:23 AM EST
Moon enters Pisces ♓ 10:41 AM EST

## TUESDAY, DECEMBER 31, 2019

## WEDNESDAY, JANUARY 1
▶ Moon void-of-course begins 9:13 PM EST
Moon enters Aries ♈ 11:00 PM EST

## THURSDAY, JANUARY 2
◑ First Quarter 11:45 PM EST

## FRIDAY, JANUARY 3
▶ Moon void-of-course begins 8:18 PM EST

## SATURDAY, JANUARY 4
Moon enters Taurus ♉ 11:15 AM EST

## SUNDAY, JANUARY 5

*Lucet & Cord weaving*

*Creating your reality. Strengthening resolve.*

# January 2020

### MONDAY, JANUARY 6
▶ Moon void-of-course begins 7:07 AM EST
Moon enters Gemini ♊ 9:10 PM EST

### TUESDAY, JANUARY 7

### WEDNESDAY, JANUARY 8
▶ Moon void-of-course begins 5:15 PM EST

### THURSDAY, JANUARY 9
Moon enters Cancer ♋ 3:43 AM EST

### FRIDAY, JANUARY 10
○ Full Moon 2:21 PM EST
▶ Moon void-of-course begins 6:58 PM EST
⛢ Uranus goes Direct 6:27 PM

### SATURDAY, JANUARY 11
Moon enters Leo ♌ 7:15 AM EST

### SUNDAY, JANUARY 12

*Hematite*

*Grounding*

- Knot Magic -
*Tying Knots - Creating*
*Untying Knots - Releasing*

# January 2020

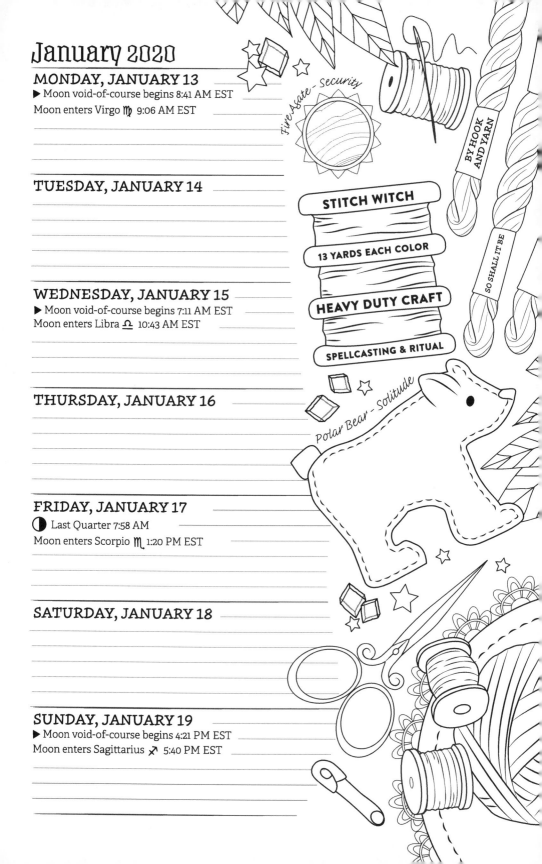

## MONDAY, JANUARY 13
▶ Moon void-of-course begins 8:41 AM EST
Moon enters Virgo ♍ 9:06 AM EST

## TUESDAY, JANUARY 14

## WEDNESDAY, JANUARY 15
▶ Moon void-of-course begins 7:11 AM EST
Moon enters Libra ♎ 10:43 AM EST

## THURSDAY, JANUARY 16

## FRIDAY, JANUARY 17
◑ Last Quarter 7:58 AM
Moon enters Scorpio ♏ 1:20 PM EST

## SATURDAY, JANUARY 18

## SUNDAY, JANUARY 19
▶ Moon void-of-course begins 4:21 PM EST
Moon enters Sagittarius ♐ 5:40 PM EST

Fire Agate - Security

BY HOOK AND YARN

SO SHALL IT BE

STITCH WITCH

13 YARDS EACH COLOR

HEAVY DUTY CRAFT

SPELLCASTING & RITUAL

Polar Bear - Solitude

# January 2020

**MONDAY, JANUARY 20**
✿ Sun enters Aquarius ♒
▶ Moon void-of-course begins 11:45 PM EST

**TUESDAY, JANUARY 21**
Moon enters Capricorn ♑ 11:59 PM EST

**WEDNESDAY, JANUARY 22**

**THURSDAY, JANUARY 23**
▶ Moon void-of-course begins 9:08 PM EST

**FRIDAY, JANUARY 24**
Moon enters Aquarius ♒ 8:20 AM EST
● New Moon 4:41 PM EST

**SATURDAY, JANUARY 25**
▶ Moon void-of-course begins 2:06 PM EST

**SUNDAY, JANUARY 26**
Moon enters Pisces ♓ 6:43 PM EST

*Narwhal*

*Singing the song of your heart*

*Walrus - Fierce Individuality*

# January · February 2020

## MONDAY, JANUARY 27

## TUESDAY, JANUARY 28
▶ Moon void-of-course begins 8:08 PM EST

## WEDNESDAY, JANUARY 29
Moon enters Aries ♈ 6:50 AM EST

## THURSDAY, JANUARY 30

## FRIDAY, JANUARY 31
▶ Moon void-of-course begins 10:09 AM EST
Moon enters Taurus ♉ 7:27 PM EST

## SATURDAY, FEBRUARY 1
☆ IMBOLC
*Fixed Festival Date
◗ First Quarter 8:41 PM EST

## SUNDAY, FEBRUARY 2

*Walnuts - Health & Power*

*Pecans - Prosperity*

**VIGOR**
Lemon, Ginger, Honey, Turmeric, Rosemary

**Health**
Pine & Cinnamon

**Happiness**
Thyme, Cherry, Lime, Cranberry

INTUITION:

Carnelian - Grounding

REFLECTION:

VISION & INTENTION:

IMPORTANT THINGS:

GOALS:

Mushroom Pie - Enhancing your Magical Powers
Crescent Rolls - The Mysteries of Emotion & Intuition

# February

## Storm Moon

Garnet – Regeneration
Quail – Awareness
Ivy – Protection & Luck
Snowdrop – Renewal

# MOON ENERGY AND SPELL IDEAS

NEW & WAXING MOON: Increasing awareness of your shadow self and subconscious.
FULL MOON: Divining messages from dreams and emotions. Reawakening visions.
WANING & DARK MOON: Purification, clearing, and cleansing of emotions and space.

*Energy Clearing & Purification*

COPAL

Clove

VETIVERT

Cedar

Sase

# CANDLE CRAFT
## BRIGHT MAGIC FOR THE DARK OF WINTER

Winter magic often focuses on celebrating light amidst the darkness, as a flickering candle casts dramatic shadows that dance in contrast to the flame.

Candles evoke a sense of mysticism, romance, and spirit. They represent the balance of dark and light and also all four elements—fire in the flame, water in the melted wax, earth in the hardened wax, and air in the smoke.

You can craft candles "from scratch" with melted wax and wicks, or you can procure them store-bought to customize and consecrate. (Use coconut, soy, beeswax, bayberry, or another "natural" wax if possible.)

OILS: Anoint your candles by rubbing a drop or two of essential oil along the length.

HERBS: Roll an oiled candle in finely crushed herbs, or add herbs to the wax if you craft your candles from scratch.

CARVING: Use a heat gun or a hair dryer to 'just' soften the wax on the side of a candle. Then carve sigils, symbols, words, or whatever markings you like.

COLOR: The color of the wax can be an important factor in candle magic, however white candles can "work" for any intention.

STONES and METALS: Place small stones or metal objects in or around your candles to evoke their energies.

INVOCATIONS: "Charge" your candles with intention—to bring light, clarity, and strength to you anytime you are facing the darkness or to help you see the opportunities and potential that are before you.

*Dragon's Blood*
*Protection, Vitality, & Power*

*Beryl*
*New Beginnings*

# Imbolc

*Brigid's Spring Water Healing & Renewal*

*Winter Jasmine Welcoming Spring*

## POWER IN THE DARKNESS
### MAGIC TO PREPARE FOR SPRING

Keeping faith in anticipation of the coming spring is a potent theme for Imbolc, a festival which celebrates the emergence from darkness into the light of the sun.

Brigid, a Celtic goddess whose name roughly translates to "fiery arrow" or "bright one," is the star of many Imbolc traditions. She represents many forms of creation and manifestation in the mundane world and is often seen at the hearth.

ENCHANT A CLOAK OR CAULDRON:

"Brigid's Mantle," or cloak, is a cloth that brings health and assists in manifestation magic.

To make your own magical cloak, gather a shawl, cloak, blanket, or piece of fabric on the eve of Imbolc. Place it on your doorstep, altar, or hearth. Brigid will pass by overnight and enchant the fabric—filling it with her blessings for the coming year. Wear your enchanted cloak for rituals, spells, or anytime you need extra power.

You can also enchant a cast-iron object such as a favorite skillet or cauldron—either using the same method as the cloak, or by leaving it overnight (with extreme caution) in a ritual fire.

CLEANSE YOUR SACRED SPACE:

An altar is a space to center your spiritual practice and bring the unseen to earth. Create or rearrange your altar with elements that signify both the darkness and the light in balance. Include items that symbolize your own sense of personal power.

Imbolc is an excellent time to consecrate, recharge, and rededicate your magical tools, crystals, and divination tools by passing them through a candle flame or herbal incense smoke.

# February 2020

| SUNDAY | MONDAY | TUESDAY |
|---|---|---|
| 26 | 27 | 28 |
| 2 | 3 | 4 ✿ IMBOLC *Astronomical Date |
| 9 ○ Full Moon | 10 | 11 |
| 16 | 17 | 18 |
| 23 ● New Moon | 24 | 25 |

| WEDNESDAY | THURSDAY | FRIDAY | SATURDAY |
|---|---|---|---|
| 29 | 30 | 31 | ☆ **IMBOLC**<br>*Fixed Festival Date<br>1 ◐ First Quarter |
| 5 | 6 | 7 | 8 |
| 12 | 13 | 14 | 15 ◑ Last Quarter |
| 19 | 20 | 21 | 22 |
| 26 | 27 | 28 | 29 |

*swan*  *grace*

# February 2020

*Hellebore*
*Protection & Banishing*

## MONDAY, FEBRUARY 3
▶ Moon void-of-course begins 6:27 AM EST
Moon enters Gemini Ⅱ 6:28 AM EST

## TUESDAY, FEBRUARY 4
☆ **IMBOLC** 3:55 AM EST
*Astronomical Date

## WEDNESDAY, FEBRUARY 5
▶ Moon void-of-course begins 9:19 AM EST
Moon enters Cancer ♋ 2:02 PM EST

## THURSDAY, FEBRUARY 6

## FRIDAY, FEBRUARY 7
▶ Moon void-of-course begins 10:42 AM EST
Moon enters Leo ♌ 5:44 PM EST

## SATURDAY, FEBRUARY 8

## SUNDAY, FEBRUARY 9
○ Full Moon 2:23 AM EST
▶ Moon void-of-course begins 11:08 AM EST
Moon enters Virgo ♍ 6:38 PM EST

**BIRTH**

What am I curious
to explore or create?

**LIFE**

What gifts have I
already received?

**DEATH**

What do I desire to
clear out or release?

# February 2020

*Mushrooms Magical Power*

## MONDAY, FEBRUARY 10

## TUESDAY, FEBRUARY 11
▶ Moon void-of-course begins 1:25 PM EST
Moon enters Libra ♎ 6:37 PM EST

## WEDNESDAY, FEBRUARY 12

## THURSDAY, FEBRUARY 13
▶ Moon void-of-course begins 4:40 PM EST
Moon enters Scorpio ♏ 7:37 PM EST

## FRIDAY, FEBRUARY 14

## SATURDAY, FEBRUARY 15
◗ Last Quarter 5:17 PM EST
▶ Moon void-of-course begins 5:19 PM EST
Moon enters Sagittarius ♐ 11:06 PM EST

## SUNDAY, FEBRUARY 16
☿℞ Mercury Retrograde 7:53 PM - March 9th, 2020

# February 2020

*Heather*
*Protection & Luck*

## MONDAY, FEBRUARY 17

## TUESDAY, FEBRUARY 18
▶ Moon void-of-course begins 4:03 AM EST
Moon enters Capricorn ♑ 5:36 AM EST
☼ Sun enters Pisces ♓

## WEDNESDAY, FEBRUARY 19

## THURSDAY, FEBRUARY 20
▶ Moon void-of-course begins 9:18 AM EST
Moon enters Aquarius ♒ 2:41 PM EST

## FRIDAY, FEBRUARY 21
▶ Moon void-of-course begins 11:08 PM EST

## SATURDAY, FEBRUARY 22

## SUNDAY, FEBRUARY 23
Moon enters Pisces ♓ 1:37 AM EST
● New Moon 10:31 AM EST

Violet - Love

Primrose - Affection

Moon Butter - Soothing Emotions

# February/March 2020

## MONDAY, FEBRUARY 24

## TUESDAY, FEBRUARY 25
▶ Moon void-of-course begins 9:11 AM EST
Moon enters Aries ♈ 1:47 PM EST

## WEDNESDAY, FEBRUARY 26

## THURSDAY, FEBRUARY 27
▶ Moon void-of-course begins 10:24 PM EST

## FRIDAY, FEBRUARY 28
Moon enters Taurus ♉ 2:29 AM EST

## SATURDAY, FEBRUARY 29

## SUNDAY, MARCH 1
▶ Moon void-of-course begins 10:52 AM EST
Moon enters Gemini ♊ 2:20 PM EST

Seeded Crackers - New Life

Herbal Butters - Health & Nourishment

Dill - Vigor

Wild Mustard - Power

Rosemary - Protection

Braided Bread - The Cycle of Life & Death

The Balance of Dark & Light

BROWN BUTTER & VINEGAR

Dandelion Greens - Divination

INTUITION: _____
_____
_____

REFLECTION: _____
_____
_____
_____
_____
_____

VISION & INTENTION: _____
_____
_____
_____

IMPORTANT THINGS: _____
_____
_____
_____
_____

GOALS: _____
_____
_____
_____

RHUBARB
ANGELICA-GINGER

CRANBERRY-ORANGE
Marmalade

LEMON-SAGE
CURD

*Affirmation:*
I am excited to bring
new energy into my life.

- Crescent Moon Scones -

- Nourishing Your Emotions -

# MARCH

*Calla Lily - Strength    Irish Moss - Luck & Abundance*

*Amber - Revitalization*

# SEED MOON

## MOON ENERGY AND SPELL IDEAS

NEW & WAXING MOON: Growing things, starting new projects, and planning for success.
FULL MOON:  Setting intentions and visualizing the outcome, taking action, making change.
WANING & DARK MOON: Banishing anxiety or cynicism about change and starting new things.

Boar - Strength

What do you see in the steam of your tea?

Blow an alder whistle or ring a bell
to summon the element of air.

*Robin – Renewal*

# SCRYING WITH AIR
## LISTENING TO THE WISDOM ON THE WIND

*If you need more information, read the **Scrying & Divination Basics** in the intro of this book!*

What energies are blowing your way as the seasons shift to spring? Spring is associated with the element of Air as well as knowledge, wisdom, communications, and things that travel "on the wind," like sounds, voices, whispers, smoke, and birds. Air is also found in your own breath—the unseen force that propels your earthly being.

SKY: Gaze out into a patch of sky. Allow yourself uninterrupted time for your focus to blur—then look for patterns, shapes, and diffusions of light.

CLOUDS: What do you see in the clouds? Cloud scrying is best on days where the clouds shift rapidly and with great enthusiasm.

SMOKE: Watch the smoke unfurl from a ritual flame, a few leaves of burning herbs, a smoky candle, or a stick of incense. Some diviners use the direction and quality of the smoke to find meaning, while some watch for shapes, letters, or symbols to appear.

WIND: Find a good windy spot and ask the spirit of air to talk to you or provide guidance. Feel and listen closely as the wind blows.

VOICE: Take note of coincidental messages "on the wind" in the form of audio or voice—snippets of timely words, synchronicities, or things you overhear in conversation. Listen closely if you suddenly get a brilliant idea "out of nowhere" or hear the call of inspiration.

BOOKS OR BIBLIOMANCY: Pick a book that you are drawn to. Open it to whatever page the book wants, and see what messages are revealed.

Awen – Inherent Creative Power

The 3 Drops of Inspiration from Cerridwen's Cauldron

# Epic Broom Ride
## Visualize Your Most Magical Self

On the Spring Equinox, journey through the veil of consciousness into whatever life you desire—in true witch style—on a broom.

The identity of "Witch" gives you the power to transform. This strength is especially potent at the Spring Equinox (Ostara) where seasonal energies are clambering to make things grow.

Prepare: Reflect on who you would be as your highest and best self. Picture it and write it down. (Dedicated! Contributing! Studious! Loving! Confident! Aligned with your best self!)

Things You'll Need: A ceremonial broom (optional). A cauldron of incense for visioning and dreams such as mugwort, rose, or angelica.

Cast the Spell: Sit comfortably with your broom nearby. Light your cauldron. Grasp the broom and close your eyes. If you're called to stand instead—do so. Say whatever words you desire, perhaps something like,

*With the power of my mind's eye*
*Let me move forward, let this broom fly!*

In the theatre of your mind, stride your broom and fling yourself up into the air. Shoot through time and space in whatever direction you like, into the future of you—your highest self.

Witness yourself flying over any obstacles or fears. You may see scenes or craggy black rocks beneath you. Fly over it, moving past at will.

Then, slow your broom and look down to see your highest self joyfully living the life of your dreams below you. Fly down and merge with this version of you, the best and most magical iteration of you that you can imagine.

Then, fly home with a renewed sense of self. Envision the route back to where you began. Open your eyes. Ground yourself, and make sure to write notes about what you saw on your broom ride, and who you became on the journey.

# March 2020

| SUNDAY | MONDAY | TUESDAY |
|--------|--------|---------|
| 1 | 2 ◑ First Quarter | 3 |
| 8 | 9 ○ Full Moon | 10 |
| 15 | 16 ◐ Last Quarter | 17 |
| 22 | 23 | 24 ● New Moon |
| 29 | 30 | 31 |

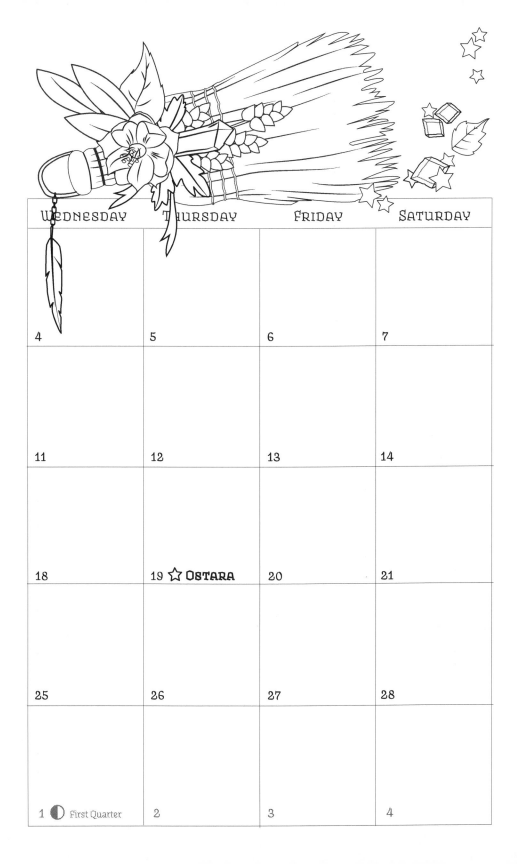

| WEDNESDAY | THURSDAY | FRIDAY | SATURDAY |
|---|---|---|---|
| 4 | 5 | 6 | 7 |
| 11 | 12 | 13 | 14 |
| 18 | 19 ☆ **OSTARA** | 20 | 21 |
| 25 | 26 | 27 | 28 |
| 1 ◖ First Quarter | 2 | 3 | 4 |

# March 2020

## MONDAY, MARCH 2
◑ First Quarter 2:57 PM EST

*Calcite*
*Energetic & Mental Prowess*

## TUESDAY, MARCH 3
▶ Moon void-of-course begins 9:19 PM EST
Moon enters Cancer ♋ 11:25 PM EST

## WEDNESDAY, MARCH 4

## THURSDAY, MARCH 5

## FRIDAY, MARCH 6
▶ Moon void-of-course begins 2:11 AM EST
Moon enters Leo ♌ 4:27 AM EST

## SATURDAY, MARCH 7

## SUNDAY, MARCH 8
▶ Moon void-of-course begins 4:12 AM EST
Moon enters Virgo ♍ 6:47 AM EST

# March 2020

## MONDAY, MARCH 9
○ Full Moon 1:47 PM EST
☿ Mercury goes Direct 11:41 PM

## TUESDAY, MARCH 10
▶ Moon void-of-course begins 4:32 AM EST
Moon enters Libra ♎ 6:02 AM EST

## WEDNESDAY, MARCH 11

## THURSDAY, MARCH 12
▶ Moon void-of-course begins 4:11 AM EST
Moon enters Scorpio ♏ 5:28 AM EST

## FRIDAY, MARCH 13

## SATURDAY, MARCH 14
▶ Moon void-of-course begins 6:05 AM EST
Moon enters Sagittarius ♐ 7:09 AM EST

## SUNDAY, MARCH 15

# March 2020

## MONDAY, MARCH 16
◑ Last Quarter 5:34 AM EST
▶ Moon void-of-course begins 5:34 AM EST
Moon enters Capricorn ♑ 12:25 PM EST

## TUESDAY, MARCH 17

## WEDNESDAY, MARCH 18
▶ Moon void-of-course begins 8:47 PM EST
Moon enters Aquarius ♒ 9:15 PM EST

## THURSDAY, MARCH 19
☆ Ostara - Spring Equinox 11:50 PM EST
✹ Sun enters Aries ♈

## FRIDAY, MARCH 20
▶ Moon void-of-course begins 4:59 AM EST

## SATURDAY, MARCH 21
Moon enters Pisces ♓ 8:33 AM EST

## SUNDAY, MARCH 22

Natural Egg Dyes

Saffron

Beets

Red Onion

Turmeric

Parsley

Blueberries

Spinach

# March 2020

## MONDAY, MARCH 23
▶ Moon void-of-course begins 10:51 AM EST
Moon enters Aries ♈ 8:57 PM EST

## TUESDAY, MARCH 24
● New Moon 5:28 AM EST

## WEDNESDAY, MARCH 25

## THURSDAY, MARCH 26
▶ Moon void-of-course begins 3:16 AM EST
Moon enters Taurus ♉ 9:36 AM EST

## FRIDAY, MARCH 27

## SATURDAY, MARCH 28
▶ Moon void-of-course begins 7:04 PM EST
Moon enters Gemini ♊ 9:37 PM EST

## SUNDAY, MARCH 29

*Draw symbols with crayons before dyeing your eggs*

*Carrot*

*Crone's Cup DARK Coffee*

*Red Wine*

# March/April 2020

## MONDAY, MARCH 30
▶ Moon void-of-course begins 11:10 AM EST

## TUESDAY, MARCH 31
Moon enters Cancer ♋ 7:43 AM EST

## WEDNESDAY, APRIL 1
◐ First Quarter 6:21 AM EST

## THURSDAY, APRIL 2
▶ Moon void-of-course begins 12:48 PM EST
Moon enters Leo ♌ 2:26 PM EST

## FRIDAY, APRIL 3
▶ Moon void-of-course begins 3:28 PM EST

## SATURDAY, APRIL 4
Moon enters Virgo ♍ 5:18 PM EST

## SUNDAY, APRIL 5

Golden Topaz
Recharging Your Spirit

Fiddleheads – New Opportunities

Radish – Visor

Pea Pods – Abundance

Gnome – Luck

Sprouts – New Life

Green Selenite – Positive Energy

Affirmation:
I am powerful, energized, and aligned with my true spirit.

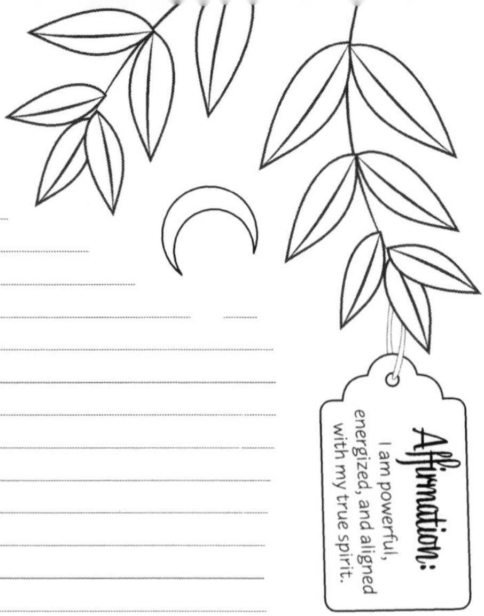

## Intuition:

## Reflection:

## Vision & Intention:

## Important Things:

## Goals:

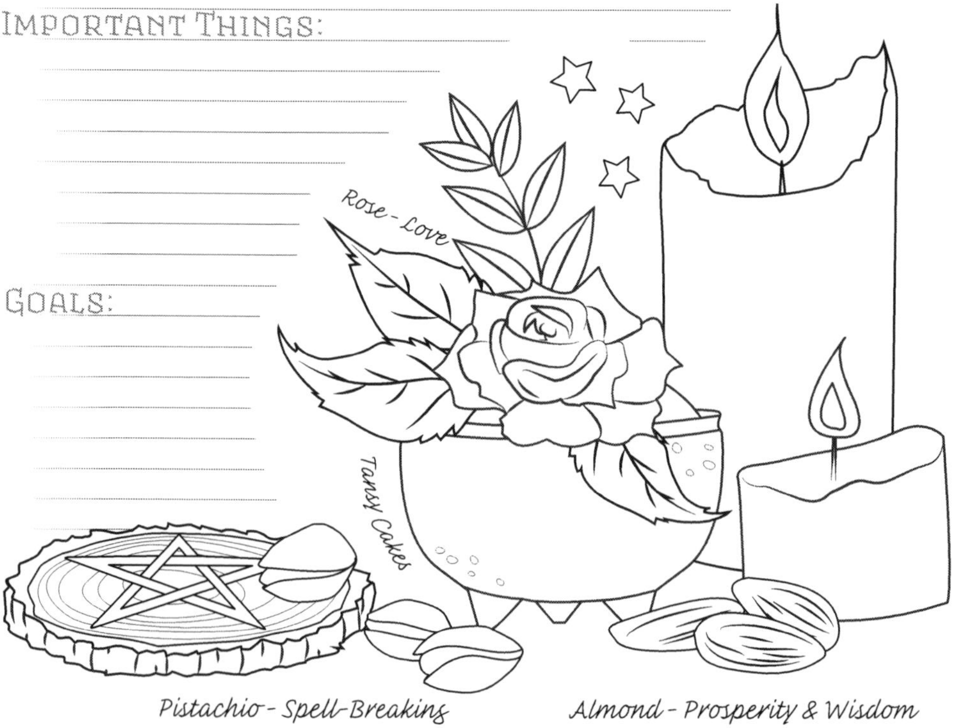

Rose - Love
Tansy Cakes
Pistachio - Spell-Breaking
Almond - Prosperity & Wisdom

# April

Peridot – Moving Forward

Moss Pink – Harmony

Peony – Energetic & Psychic Protection

Frog – Transformation

# Pink Moon

## MOON ENERGY AND SPELL IDEAS

NEW & WAXING MOON: Starting new projects, taking action, and following your curiosity.
FULL MOON: Energy, strength, growth, happiness, and resurrection of your true self.
WANING & DARK MOON: Reflecting on self-doubt and inaction, then banishing any issues.

Geranium
Protection, Health,
& Friendship

# A Witch's Garden

## Growing Your Magic on Earth and in Spirit

April bursts forth with a powerful and deeply spiritual essence of new life. It can feel awesome, yet also chaotic and unsettling, like the wild energy of the wind and of the sun in Aries.

When we see growth on plants, it's exciting, but when it comes to personal growth, change can feel disjointing and unsure. In fact, the unconscious mind assumes "change" means "danger" and alerts you by creating anxiety... even if the "change" is something you want.

And so, you can use the "growth" energy of gardening (even just one small houseplant) to nurture yourself through changes. The energy of plants can help you shift your thoughts from the fears and doubts that often come with personal growth, to witnessing your magic, wonder, and progress instead.

Go as far into "gardening-as-witchcraft" as you like — plant trees, create an outdoor altar, labyrinth, pentagonal herb plot, an eight-pieced wheel, or an old cauldron filled with flowers.

Once you've planted or anytime you see fit, have a candlelit procession or ceremony. Dedicate yourself to tend to the garden's well-being and growth as you go forth in your own personal development.

Then as you care for your plant(s) in the coming weeks, feel the energy of their growth. Watch them take root and witness the sense of sacred power that breathes life into all things. Feel that same power inside of yourself and visualize however you wish to be. In time, you'll naturally find that you connect to your highest self whenever you tend to your garden.

# April 2020

| | SUNDAY | MONDAY | TUESDAY |
|---|---|---|---|
| | 29 | 30 | 31 |
| | 5 | 6 | 7 ⚪ Full Moon |
| | 12 | 13 | 14 ◑ Last Quarter |
| | 19 | 20 | 21 |
| | 26 | 27 | 28 |

Grow rosemary to attract elves.

| WEDNESDAY | THURSDAY | FRIDAY | SATURDAY |
|---|---|---|---|
| 1 ◑ First Quarter | 2 | 3 | 4 |
| 8 | 9 | 10 | 11 |
| 15 | 16 | 17 | 18 |
| 22 ● New Moon | 23 | 24 | 25 |
| 29 | 30 ◑ First Quarter | 1 | 2 |

# April 2020

## MONDAY, APRIL 6
▶ Moon void-of-course begins 9:28 AM EST
Moon enters Libra ♎ 5:16 PM EST

## TUESDAY, APRIL 7
○ Full Moon 10:34 PM EST

## WEDNESDAY, APRIL 8
▶ Moon void-of-course begins 8:49 AM EST
Moon enters Scorpio ♏ 4:16 PM EST

## THURSDAY, APRIL 9

## FRIDAY, APRIL 10
▶ Moon void-of-course begins 3:34 PM EST
Moon enters Sagittarius ♐ 4:35 PM EST

## SATURDAY, APRIL 11

## SUNDAY, APRIL 12
▶ Moon void-of-course begins 7:45 AM EST
Moon enters Capricorn ♑ 8:05 PM EST

# April 2020

## MONDAY, APRIL 13

## TUESDAY, APRIL 14
◗ Last Quarter 6:56 PM EST
▶ Moon void-of-course begins 7:47 PM EST

## WEDNESDAY, APRIL 15
Moon enters Aquarius ♒ 3:36 AM EST

## THURSDAY, APRIL 16

## FRIDAY, APRIL 17
▶ Moon void-of-course begins 10:34 AM EST
Moon enters Pisces ♓ 2:29 PM EST

## SATURDAY, APRIL 18

## SUNDAY, APRIL 19
▶ Moon void-of-course begins 7:30 PM EST
✿ Sun enters Taurus ♉

# April 2020

## MONDAY, APRIL 20
Moon enters Aries ♈ 3:00 AM EST

*Clear Quartz*
*Channeling Energy*

## TUESDAY, APRIL 21

## WEDNESDAY, APRIL 22
▶ Moon void-of-course begins 8:31 AM EST
Moon enters Taurus ♉ 3:35 PM EST
● New Moon 10:25 PM EST

*Tin*
*Elves & Prosperity*

## THURSDAY, APRIL 23

## FRIDAY, APRIL 24
▶ Moon void-of-course begins 8:42 PM EST

## SATURDAY, APRIL 25
Moon enters Gemini ♊ 3:19 AM EST
♀℞ Pluto Retrograde 9:58 AM - Oct. 4th 2020

## SUNDAY, APRIL 26

MOONHARE'S
INCREDIBLY RARE & RABBITY

Nettle Tea
Nettle - Red Clover - Lemon Balm - Parsley

# April/May 2020

## MONDAY, APRIL 27
▶ Moon void-of-course begins 12:59 PM EST
Moon enters Cancer ♋ 1:27 PM EST

## TUESDAY, APRIL 28

## WEDNESDAY, APRIL 29
▶ Moon void-of-course begins 3:29 PM EST
Moon enters Leo ♌ 9:06 PM EST

## THURSDAY, APRIL 30
◗ First Quarter 4:38 PM EST

## FRIDAY, MAY 1
▶ Moon void-of-course begins 12:04 PM EST
☆ Beltane
*Fixed Festival Date

## SATURDAY, MAY 2
Moon enters Virgo ♍ 1:35 AM EST

## SUNDAY, MAY 3
▶ Moon void-of-course begins 10:24 PM EST

Gold – The Sun

Silver – The Moon

Opal – Vision & Creativity

Rabbit – Action

Egg – New Life

# INTUITION:

_____

_____

_____

_____

_____

# REFLECTION:

_____

_____

_____

_____

_____

**Affirmation:**
I love and forgive
myself (and others).

# VISION & INTENTION:

_____

_____

_____

_____

_____

# IMPORTANT THINGS:

_____

_____

_____

_____

# GOALS:

_____

_____

_____

_____

Maple

Life-Force Energy

Lemon - Happiness

# MAY

*Ruby in Fuchsite - Creating Positive Energy*

*Orchid - Love*

# FLOWER MOON

## MOON ENERGY AND SPELL IDEAS

NEW & WAXING MOON: Attracting love, passion, abundance, and increasing your vitality.
FULL MOON: Igniting your power, bringing your dreams to life, cultivating your spirituality.
WANING & DARK MOON: Banishing fears and releasing resentment towards those you love.

Inspiration
How can I stoke the fires of my imagination?

Nature
What message does the natural world wish for me to hear?

Wisdom
What am I missing that the wise faeries can see?

Faerie Tarot

*Look through a holey stone to see the faerie realm*

VIOLET WINE

BUTTERMILK

HONEY

# Faerie Magic & Friendships
## Inviting Faeries to Spells and Rituals

Faerie Folk (or Faery, Fairy, Fae, amongst other names) are timeless beings that are known in many forms and traditions, in all dimensions of space and existence.

Working with faeries is a bit like working with deities—you're asking for their powers and presence—and they can be temperamental—so there are some rules and protections that are wise to put in place (*A Witch's Guide to Faery Folk* by Edain McCoy offers a lot of wisdom on this).

If you are patient and kind, you can learn to see faeries, build a relationship with them, and, eventually, invite them to perform magic with you. Faerie magic is excellent for things like protecting your home and garden, helping plants grow, communicating with animals, channeling creative inspiration, raising energy, divination,

and calling upon higher or ancient wisdom for guidance.

To invite faeries to a spell, cast a strong circle of protection and use any herbs, stones, or other precautions that you desire (a bell will scare off any faerie, malevolent or otherwise). State the intention for your spell and make sure your energy is fun and lively. Then invite the faeries to join you. Song and dance will encourage them, however, never demand anything of faeries—simply invite them, and let them choose.

Make sure to leave an offering anytime you reach out to faeries. Cake, candy, milk, butter, wine, bread, or shiny stones, bits of silk, ribbon, buttons, flowers, and small pieces of lumber are all fabulous offerings (if you don't want to build them a tiny house!).

FIG-RAISIN-HONEY

CHERRY-CINNAMON-CARAMEL

VANILLA-MAPLE

# Bannock

COOK A MAGICAL OAT CAKE AND CAST A SPELL FOR PROSPERITY

**Beltane**

Hazel - Wisdom · Holly - Peace · Oak - Endurance · Rowan - Power · Willow - Intuition

Hawthorn - Magic · Birch - Renewal · Alder - Protection · Ash - Prosperity

NINE WOODS OF THE BELTANE FIRE

# BELTANE FESTIVITIES
## SPELLS AND MAGIC TO LIGHT YOUR FIRE

Beltane is the celebration of the return to the light half of the year (the "big sun" or summer in Celtic terms). Flowers, frolicking, fire, fertility rites, luck, power, and high-spirited festivities were common on Beltane, as were eating traditional oat cakes called bannock.

DECORATIONS: A maypole may be iconic, but the "maybush" was even more common in ancient practice. Typically a hawthorn branch, the maybush was decorated in friendly competition—much like a Yule tree—with candles, ribbons, ornaments, beads, shells, and feathers.

SPELLWORK: Tie ribbons as "wishes" onto a tree or branch. Use symbolic colors or just cast the wish by holding the ribbon and setting an intention. As your ribbon blows in the wind, the wishes will be cast out into the universe. If you continue to vibrate the energy of the wish you desire — it'll come back to you in "real life!"

On Beltane eve, dance, chant or otherwise circle around your maybush to celebrate the never-ending spirit of life and abundance. At the end of the night, burn your maybush as a symbolic act of fiery power. You can also cast flowers (and wishes) into a ritual fire or dress a single candle with oil and crushed herbs.

FOOD: Traditional bannock oak cakes were cooked over an open flame in the bottom of a cauldron or skillet—then split into equal pieces, one for everyone in attendance.

You can make your oat cake either savory or sweet, depending on what you add to it. (See suggestions on the facing page.)

# May 2020

| Sunday | Monday | Tuesday |
|--------|--------|---------|
| 26 | 27 | 28 |
| 3 | **☼ Beltane** 4 *Astronomical Date | 5 |
| 10 | 11 | 12 |
| 17 | 18 | 19 |
| 24 | 25 | 26 |
| 31 | 1 | 2 |

*Copper & Red Coral – Love, Luck, & Healing*

| WEDNESDAY | THURSDAY | FRIDAY | SATURDAY |
|---|---|---|---|
| 29 | 30 ◐ First Quarter | ☆ **BELTANE** 1 *Fixed Festival Date | 2 |
| 6 | 7 ○ Full Moon | 8 | 9 |
| 13 | 14 ◐ Last Quarter | 15 | 16 |
| 20 | 21 | 22 ● New Moon | 23 |
| 27 | 28 | 29 ◑ First Quarter | 30 |
| 3 | 4 | 5 ○ Full Moon | 6 |

# May 2020

## MONDAY, MAY 4

Moon enters Libra ♎ 3:09 AM EST

✿ Beltane 8:49 PM EST

*Astronomical Date

## TUESDAY, MAY 5

▶ Moon void-of-course begins 10:30 PM EST

## WEDNESDAY, MAY 6

Moon enters Scorpio ♏ 3:04 AM EST

## THURSDAY, MAY 7

◯ Full Moon 6:45 AM EST

▶ Moon void-of-course begins 10:38 PM EST

## FRIDAY, MAY 8

Moon enters Sagittarius ♐ 3:15 AM EST

## SATURDAY, MAY 9

## SUNDAY, MAY 10

▶ Moon void-of-course begins 2:10 AM EST

Moon enters Capricorn ♑ 5:38 AM EST

Fruit Blossoms

Love, Friendship, & Happiness

LAVENDER SUGAR

Violet

Rose

Pansy

# May 2020

## MONDAY, MAY 11
♄℞ Saturn Retrograde 10:11 PM - Sept. 28, 2020

## TUESDAY, MAY 12
▶ Moon void-of-course begins 6:29 AM EST
Moon enters Aquarius ♒ 11:38 AM EST

## WEDNESDAY, MAY 13
♀℞ Venus Retrograde 2:44 AM - June 25, 2020

## THURSDAY, MAY 14
♃℞ Jupiter Retrograde 9:48 AM - Sept. 12, 2020
◑ Last Quarter 10:02 AM EST
▶ Moon void-of-course begins 10:02 AM EST
Moon enters Pisces ♓ 9:24 PM EST

## FRIDAY, MAY 15

## SATURDAY, MAY 16

## SUNDAY, MAY 17
▶ Moon void-of-course begins 3:59 AM EST
Moon enters Aries ♈ 9:35 AM EST

Edible FLOWERS

*Nasturtium*

*Marigold*

*Dianthus*

*Dandelion Greens*

# May 2020

## MONDAY, MAY 18

## TUESDAY, MAY 19
▶ Moon void-of-course begins 4:32 PM EST
Moon enters Taurus ♉ 10:10 PM EST

## WEDNESDAY, MAY 20
✿ Sun enters Gemini ♊

## THURSDAY, MAY 21

## FRIDAY, MAY 22
▶ Moon void-of-course begins 4:00 AM EST
Moon enters Gemini ♊ 9:35 AM EST
● New Moon 1:38 PM EST

## SATURDAY, MAY 23

## SUNDAY, MAY 24
▶ Moon void-of-course begins 7:09 AM EST
Moon enters Cancer ♋ 7:08 PM EST

# May 2020

## MONDAY, MAY 25

## TUESDAY, MAY 26
▶ Moon void-of-course begins 9:06 PM EST

## WEDNESDAY, MAY 27
Moon enters Leo ♌ 2:32 AM EST

## THURSDAY, MAY 28
▶ Moon void-of-course begins 9:30 AM EST

## FRIDAY, MAY 29
Moon enters Virgo ♍ 7:40 AM EST
◗ First Quarter 11:29 PM EST

## SATURDAY, MAY 30

## SUNDAY, MAY 31
▶ Moon void-of-course begins 5:16 AM EST
Moon enters Libra ♎ 10:37 AM EST

INTUITION:

REFLECTION:

VISION & INTENTION:

IMPORTANT THINGS:

GOALS:

Affirmation:
I know who I am, and I am strong in my own power.

Marigold Divination

Strawberry-Rhubarb Pie
Dedication to Happiness

# JUNE

*St. John's Wort – Health & Happiness*

*Aquamarine – Courage & Light*

# HONEY MOON

## MOON ENERGY AND SPELL IDEAS

NEW & WAXING MOON: Increasing confidence, abundance, and making new friends.
FULL MOON: Protection, celebrating your success, and divination for your highest self.
WANING & DARK MOON: Releasing self-doubt, perfectionism, and negative emotions.

# SCRYING WITH FIRE
## DIVINING THE WISDOM OF THE FLAMES

*If you need more information, read the **Scrying & Divination Basics** in the intro of this book!*

Summer is the season of sun and fire. Gazing into fire and seeing spirits, messages, guides, faces, and otherworldly presences, also called pyromancy, presents an accessible portal to the wisdom of the divine and to the spirit world.

FLAME GAZING: Gazing into a candle flame or pile of burning embers is a simple way to divine with fire. Sit in silence and in pitch darkness, other than the flame. Let your focus blur out and your mind clear of all chatter and thoughts. Watch the flames and see what shapes, messages, or feelings come. You can also watch the flicker of the flames and the direction of the smoke or listen to the sounds and rhythms as it burns.

SPIRIT SUMMONING: Ask to see a spirit guide's face in the fire — or ask directly for guidance and wisdom from the element of fire. This type of fire scrying can be intense—so always visualize an orb of white light around yourself first and ask for protective energy.

HERB CASTING: Cast dragon's blood into the fire and ask for guidance from your shadow side.

Toss sweetgrass into the fire and look for a message from your divine self. Throw a handful of mugwort into the fire and request to see a creative vision.

ASH SCRYING: After your midsummer bonfire (or any ceremonial fire!), take a handful of cooled ashes and toss them onto the ground. Gaze to look for any shapes or patterns that emerge. You can also gaze at the ashes as they have fallen in the firepit.

Bastet - Egyptian Goddess of the Sun, Cats, Happiness, and Pleasure

Blackthorn - The Magic of Life & Death

Juniper - Justice & Protection

Redwood - Wisdom & Growth

Poplar - Divination

Linden

Feminine Power

Bay

Masculine Power

WAND

WOODS

# Litha

# Solstice Wandcraft
## Empower Your Magic and Wand

The Summer Solstice, also known as Litha and "Midsummer" is the point of the year where the day is longest, and the sun shines at maximum strength. It is an "in-between" time of shifting seasons, and a chance to slip into another world, change your future, and rise to your full power.

It's also an excellent day to make or consecrate a wand. Traditionally, a witch would go in search of her wand's wood before dawn and follow specific customs (research if you want to do this in the old ways, otherwise, create your wand as you see fit). You can use a crystal wand, a metal scepter, something you bought, something you made, or whatever you like.

Things You'll Need: Your wand. A ritual fire or cauldron with sand at the bottom and three yellow candles within. Chamomile or fennel tea.

Dragon's blood, bay, pine, or cinquefoil incense.

Perform the Ritual: Place your wand out in the full noon sun on the solstice for at least three hours or until sunset.

Then light your cauldron or candles. Wield your wand skyward and with power as you circle the flames thirteen times, clockwise. If you have a fire, you can cast flowers or herbs into the fire. If you are using the candles, just toss a bit of herbs towards the flames as you go 'round. Meanwhile, chant (or words of your choosing):

*May this witch and wand acquire*
*The power of this solstice fire.*

As the fire burns out, sit and sip mead or chamomile tea. Pick out tarot cards that symbolize the highest version of you or gaze into the flames and embers for intuitive wisdom.

# June 2020

| | SUNDAY | MONDAY | TUESDAY |
|---|---|---|---|
| | 31 | 1 | 2 |
| | 7 | 8 | 9 |
| | 14 | 15 | 16 |
| | 21 ● New Moon | 22 | 23 |
| | 28 ◑ First Quarter | 29 | 30 |

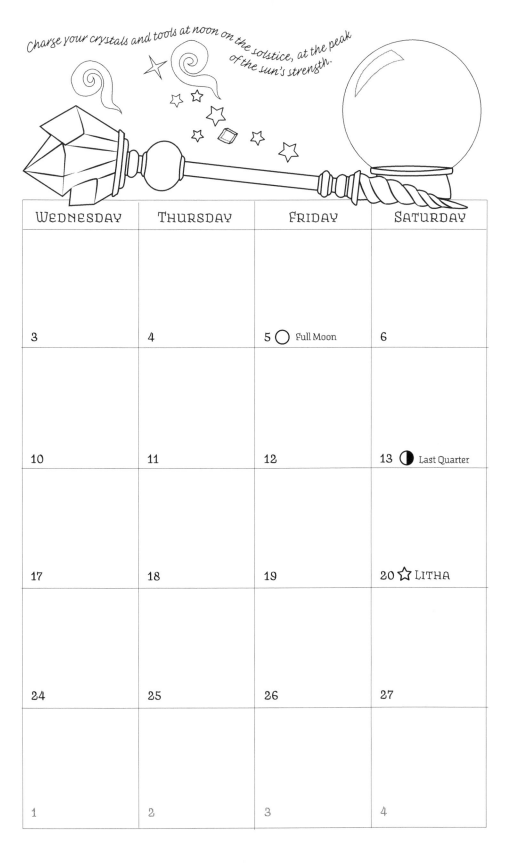

*Charge your crystals and tools at noon on the solstice, at the peak of the sun's strength.*

| WEDNESDAY | THURSDAY | FRIDAY | SATURDAY |
|---|---|---|---|
| 3 | 4 | 5 ◯ Full Moon | 6 |
| 10 | 11 | 12 | 13 ◑ Last Quarter |
| 17 | 18 | 19 | 20 ☆ LITHA |
| 24 | 25 | 26 | 27 |
| 1 | 2 | 3 | 4 |

# June 2020

**MONDAY, JUNE 1**

**TUESDAY, JUNE 2**
▶ Moon void-of-course begins 6:39 AM EST
Moon enters Scorpio ♏ 12:05 PM EST

**WEDNESDAY, JUNE 3**

**THURSDAY, JUNE 4**
▶ Moon void-of-course begins 7:36 AM EST
Moon enters Sagittarius ♐ 1:16 PM EST

**FRIDAY, JUNE 5**
○ Full Moon 3:12 PM EST

**SATURDAY, JUNE 6**
▶ Moon void-of-course begins 12:10 AM EST
Moon enters Capricorn ♑ 3:44 PM EST

**SUNDAY, JUNE 7**

Blue Topaz - Attuning to Your Highest Self

Dragonfly - Transformations & Self-Realization

Alder - Foundations & New Beginnings

# June 2020

*Sycamore - Patience*

## MONDAY, JUNE 8
▶ Moon void-of-course begins 2:05 AM EST
Moon enters Aquarius ♒ 8:53 PM EST

## TUESDAY, JUNE 9

*Jeweled Scarab Beetle*
*Transformation & Resurrection*

## WEDNESDAY, JUNE 10
▶ Moon void-of-course begins 10:34 AM EST

## THURSDAY, JUNE 11
Moon enters Pisces ♓ 5:31 AM EST

## FRIDAY, JUNE 12

*Moonstone*

## SATURDAY, JUNE 13
◗ Last Quarter 2:23 AM EST
▶ Moon void-of-course begins 8:44 AM EST
Moon enters Aries ♈ 5:02 PM EST

*Sunstone - Joy & Intuition*

*The Depths of Emotion*

## SUNDAY, JUNE 14

# June 2020

## MONDAY, JUNE 15
▶ Moon void-of-course begins 8:49 PM EST

## TUESDAY, JUNE 16
Moon enters Taurus ♉ 5:35 AM EST

## WEDNESDAY, JUNE 17

## THURSDAY, JUNE 18
☿℞ Mercury Retrograde 12:53 AM - July 12, 2020
▶ Moon void-of-course begins 8:02 AM EST
Moon enters Gemini ♊ 4:59 PM EST

## FRIDAY, JUNE 19

## SATURDAY, JUNE 20
☆ LITHA - SUMMER SOLSTICE 5:44 PM EST
▶ Moon void-of-course begins 5:47 PM EST
☼ Sun enters Cancer ♋

## SUNDAY, JUNE 21
Moon enters Cancer ♋ 2:01 AM EST
● New Moon 2:41 AM EST

# June 2020

## MONDAY, JUNE 22

## TUESDAY, JUNE 23
▶ Moon void-of-course begins 3:20 AM EST
Moon enters Leo ♌ 8:33 AM EST
♆℞ Neptune Retrograde 7:02 PM - Nov. 28, 2020

## WEDNESDAY, JUNE 24
▶ Moon void-of-course begins 1:34 AM EST

## THURSDAY, JUNE 25
♀ Venus goes Direct 2:47 AM
Moon enters Virgo ♍ 1:04 PM EST

## FRIDAY, JUNE 26

## SATURDAY, JUNE 27
▶ Moon void-of-course begins 4:01 PM EST
Moon enters Libra ♎ 4:16 PM EST

## SUNDAY, JUNE 28
◗ First Quarter 4:15 AM EST

Burn Sprigs of
GORSE
for Prosperity &
Protection

# June/July 2020

## MONDAY, JUNE 29
▶ Moon void-of-course begins 9:01 AM EST
Moon enters Scorpio ♏ 6:47 PM EST

*Dogwood – Wishes*

## TUESDAY, JUNE 30

*Blue-Green Jade
Peace & Serenity*

## WEDNESDAY, JULY 1
▶ Moon void-of-course begins 9:20 PM EST
Moon enters Sagittarius ♐ 9:20 PM EST

## THURSDAY, JULY 2

*Blue Beryl – Clarity & Focus*

## FRIDAY, JULY 3
▶ Moon void-of-course begins 9:05 AM EST

## SATURDAY, JULY 4
Moon enters Capricorn ♑ 12:47 AM EST

## SUNDAY, JULY 5
○ Full Moon 12:44 AM EST

*Donkey - Practicality & Patience*

INTUITION:

REFLECTION:

VISION & INTENTION:

IMPORTANT THINGS:

GOALS:

*Affirmation:*
I am creating my life and fulfilling my purpose.

Spirulina - Vitality

Coconut Milk - Purification

Mint - Prosperity

# July

## Thunder Moon

Malachite & Azurite - Transformation & Personal Power
Mother-of-Pearl - Health & Prosperity
Bladderwrack - Protection, Money, & Psychic Powers

## MOON ENERGY AND SPELL IDEAS

NEW & WAXING MOON: Increasing confidence in your voice, vision, and creative expression.
FULL MOON: Divination for your highest self and discovering your soul's purpose.
WANING & DARK MOON: Releasing emotional patterns that are holding back your true self.

Blue Lace Agate & Turquoise – Expression

Labradorite

Raising Consciousness

River Mud

Grounding Emotions

Sea Salt
Purification

Sea Water
New Beginnings

# MOON BATHS & SEA WITCHERY
## RITUALS WITH THE LIFE-GIVING ENERGY OF WATER

Mermaids live a life of true natural abundance. While they prefer seclusion, they aren't shy. Mermaids live on their own terms—slathered in enigmatic beauty and artful aquatic accessories. Channel the energy of mermaids with these ritual baths and simple acts of sea witchery.

OCEAN ALTAR: Summon nature's abundance with a sea altar. Fill a large glass jar or vessel with fine, clean sand. Place appropriately scented or colored candles and decorate it with shells and opulent items. Try antique pearls, gold chains and gemstones, or natural treasures like feathers, flowers, hagstones, and sea glass. Sprinkle sea water or sea salt to consecrate the energy.

Evoke the essence and scent of the beach with incense or oils. Try geranium, vetivert, cedar, and ylang-ylang with a hint of fennel or eucalyptus depending on what "the beach" smells like to you.

AQUATIC RITUALS AND MOON BATHS:

Perform these rituals in any body of water, a swimming pool, bathtub, lake, ocean, stream, or just envision them in your mind's eye.

DARK MOON THEME: To release things. Mix a sachet of sea salts, bladderwrack, lavender, and rosemary (make a shower scrub by adding shea butter or coconut oil). Submerge yourself in the water, and when you emerge, you will leave behind what you wish to release.

FULL MOON THEME: To attain wisdom or transformation. Mix a sachet of sea salts, bladderwrack, rose petals, lemon verbena, and calendula. Ask for guidance while underwater. When you emerge, you will receive an answer or find the solution. You may prefer to envision yourself how you wish to be while underwater, and when you emerge, you will have become it.

# July 2020

| | SUNDAY | MONDAY | TUESDAY |
|---|---|---|---|
| | 28 ◑ First Quarter | 29 | 30 |
| | 5 ◯ Full Moon | 6 | 7 |
| | 12 ◐ Last Quarter | 13 | 14 |
| | 19 | 20 ● New Moon | 21 |
| | 26 | 27 ◐ First Quarter | 28 |

| WEDNESDAY | THURSDAY | FRIDAY | SATURDAY |
|---|---|---|---|
| 1 | 2 | 3 | 4 |
| 8 | 9 | 10 | 11 |
| 15 | 16 | 17 | 18 |
| 22 | 23 | 24 | 25 |
| 29 | 30 | 31 | 1 |

# July 2020

*Ebb Tide (water flowing out)*
*Releasing & Removing Obstacles*

## MONDAY, JULY 6
▶ Moon void-of-course begins 5:35 AM EST
Moon enters Aquarius ♒ 6:08 AM EST

## TUESDAY, JULY 7
▶ Moon void-of-course begins 12:37 AM EST

## WEDNESDAY, JULY 8
Moon enters Pisces ♓ 2:12 PM EST

## THURSDAY, JULY 9

## FRIDAY, JULY 10
▶ Moon void-of-course begins 11:48 PM EST

## SATURDAY, JULY 11
Moon enters Aries ♈ 1:05 AM EST

*Low Tide*
*Rest, Reflection & Shadow Work*

## SUNDAY, JULY 12
☿ Mercury goes Direct 4:21 AM
◑ Last Quarter 7:28 PM EST

# July 2020

*Hang a hagstone on red string to craft a protection charm*

### MONDAY, JULY 13
▶ Moon void-of-course begins 11:54 AM EST
Moon enters Taurus ♉ 1:33 PM EST

### TUESDAY, JULY 14

### WEDNESDAY, JULY 15
▶ Moon void-of-course begins 11:21 PM EST

### THURSDAY, JULY 16
Moon enters Gemini ♊ 1:18 AM EST

### FRIDAY, JULY 17
▶ Moon void-of-course begins 5:14 PM EST

### SATURDAY, JULY 18
Moon enters Cancer ♋ 10:23 AM EST

*Seaweed Salad*
*Health & Vitality*

### SUNDAY, JULY 19

# July 2020

## MONDAY, JULY 20
● New Moon 1:32 PM EST
▶ Moon void-of-course begins 1:54 PM EST
Moon enters Leo ♌ 4:16 PM EST

## TUESDAY, JULY 21
▶ Moon void-of-course begins 8:27 PM EST

## WEDNESDAY, JULY 22
✿ Sun enters Leo
Moon enters Virgo ♍ 7:39 PM EST

## THURSDAY, JULY 23

## FRIDAY, JULY 24
▶ Moon void-of-course begins 7:07 PM EST
Moon enters Libra ♎ 9:53 PM EST

## SATURDAY, JULY 25

## SUNDAY, JULY 26
▶ Moon void-of-course begins 9:08 PM EST

Abalone - Peace & Calming

Pearl - Full Moon Magic

Coral - Protection

Sapphire - Wisdom

# July/August 2020

## MONDAY, JULY 27
Moon enters Scorpio ♏ 12:11 AM EST
◑ First Quarter 8:32 AM EST

## TUESDAY, JULY 28

## WEDNESDAY, JULY 29
▶ Moon void-of-course begins 12:01 AM EST
Moon enters Sagittarius ♐ 3:24 AM EST

## THURSDAY, JULY 30
▶ Moon void-of-course begins 8:07 PM EST

## FRIDAY, JULY 31
Moon enters Capricorn ♑ 7:58 AM EST

## SATURDAY, AUGUST 1
☆ Lughnasadh
*Fixed Festival Date

*Flow Tide (water coming in)
Increasing & Manifesting*

## SUNDAY, AUGUST 2
▶ Moon void-of-course begins 9:59 AM EST
Moon enters Aquarius ♒ 2:10 PM EST

*High Tide
Full Energy & Magical Power*

INTUITION:

_____
_____
_____
_____
_____

REFLECTION:

_____
_____
_____
_____

VISION & INTENTION:

_____
_____
_____
_____
_____

IMPORTANT THINGS:

_____
_____
_____
_____

**Affirmation:**
I am ready to see new
wisdom and insights.

Brass
Healing & Protection

GOALS:

_____
_____
_____

Blueberry & Bilberry - Protection

# AUGUST

Blackberry - Magical Powers, Health, & Abundance

Falcon - Judgment & Vision

Corn - Abundance & Protection

Raspberry - Love

# CORN MOON

## MOON ENERGY AND SPELL IDEAS

NEW & WAXING MOON: Increasing abundance, success, playfulness, and fulfillment.
FULL MOON: Connecting to your guiding light and intuition. Gratitude and protection.
WANING & DARK MOON: Releasing feelings of scarcity, unworthiness, or boredom.

Celtic Knot Patterns
Protection & Power

Bilberry Bracelet
- Love -

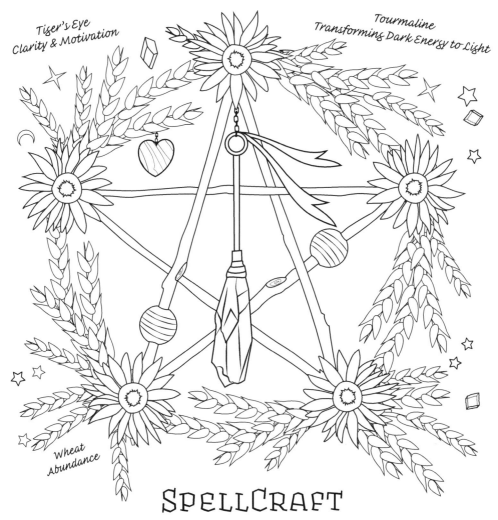

Tiger's Eye
Clarity & Motivation

Tourmaline
Transforming Dark Energy to Light

Wheat
Abundance

# SpellCraft

## Making Magic for the First Harvest

The Sun god Lugh was known to be playful in spirit and a god of "many talents and gifts," such as magic, craft, poetry, sport, and art.

Lugh represented the ability to bring things to life and participate with passion in any endeavor.

Outdoor games and sports were traditional for Lughnasadh, as was crafting and creating from the abundant elements of nature. Plants, vines, fruits, shells, feathers, sticks, and stones offer ample opportunities for seasonal witchcraft.

**CRAFT RITUALS:** Set the intention of your craft project as you plan it out. Find materials that symbolize the qualities and energy of what you desire to create in your life.

**Stitch Witchery:** Whether you sew, embroider, or do crochet or macramé, each stitch can be infused with a mantra of intention. Experiment with natural dyes and "color magic" symbolism.

**Jewelry and Adornments:** Try your hand at beading with earthy twines and accouterments. Add crystals, stones, shells, and other natural elements to create your own wearable charms.

**Fruit, Herbs, and Grains:** Corn husk dollies and braids are a traditional craft, as are garlic and onion braids which can be hung in the kitchen for protection.

**Potato Stamps:** Carve a potato with suns, moons, or Celtic knot patterns. Then use fabric paint to stamp bands of spellwork at the hems of dish towels, aprons, an altar cloth, special paper, or whatever you like.

**Besoms, Wands, Stangs, and Staffs:** Collect sticks, twigs, and auspicious pieces of wood to make your own magical tools.

Basil & Dill
Protection & Abundance

Cat - Magic

# Lughnasadh

Owl - Otherworldly Wisdom

## Ritual Bread
### Giving Thanks for the Earth's Abundance

Lughnasadh, also called Lammas, is the "First Harvest" festival of grain, corn, herbs, fruits, and vegetables. Consuming the ritual bread and beer was celebratory, but more importantly, a ritual of faith that the coming harvests would be bountiful enough to last through winter.

The first grain signified the mystery of life and death and the cyclical connection of our food to the elements and earthly divine.

BREAD RITUALS: While you bake or prepare your bread, think about your connection to the ingredients and feel gratitude for the abundance that the earth provides.

As you break your bread, give thanks to the sun, the earth, and the great spirit (or whoever you work with) for your life on earth. Ask for a blessing into the dark season as winter falls.

You can also follow the "First Loaf" tradition by making a small loaf "first" to offer on your altar or to feed to the birds.

SHAPES: Shape your Lughnasadh bread into suns or "men" to represent the traditional sacrifice of the Sun King Lugh and the harvest of grains. You can also create spirals, wheels, braids, animals, or any other shapes or symbols that you desire.

HERBAL SPELLS AND ADDITIONS: To add festive kitchen magic to your bread, add crushed herbs to the dough or press leaves into the tops of your loaves before baking. Try dill, marjoram, and oregano for happiness; lavender, honey, and thyme for peace and tranquility; or caraway, red pepper flakes, and roasted garlic for magical strength, vitality, and power.

# August 2020

| | SUNDAY | MONDAY | TUESDAY |
|---|---|---|---|
| | 26 | 27 ◑ First Quarter | 28 |
| | 2 | 3 ◯ Full Moon | 4 |
| | 9 | 10 | 11 ◐ Last Quarter |
| | 16 | 17 | 18 ● New Moon |
| | 23 | 24 | 25 ◐ First Quarter |
| | 30 | 31 | 1 |

| WEDNESDAY | THURSDAY | FRIDAY | SATURDAY |
|-----------|----------|--------|----------|
| 29 | 30 | 31 | 1 ☆ **LUGHNASADH** *Fixed Festival Date |
| 5 | 6 ✿ **LUGHNASADH** *Astronomical Date | 7 | 8 |
| 12 | 13 | 14 | 15 |
| 19 | 20 | 21 | 22 |
| 26 | 27 | 28 | 29 |
| 2 ◯ Full Moon | 3 | 4 | 5 |

# August 2020

**MONDAY, AUGUST 3**

○ Full Moon 11:59 AM EST

*Zucchini Abundance*

*Tomato Prosperity*

**TUESDAY, AUGUST 4**

▶ Moon void-of-course begins 5:45 PM EST
Moon enters Pisces ♓ 10:27 PM EST

**WEDNESDAY, AUGUST 5**

**THURSDAY, AUGUST 6**

✿ **Lughnasadh** 9:04 PM EST
*Astronomical Date

**FRIDAY, AUGUST 7**

▶ Moon void-of-course begins 8:53 AM EST
Moon enters Aries ♈ 9:04 AM EST

**SATURDAY, AUGUST 8**

**SUNDAY, AUGUST 9**

▶ Moon void-of-course begins 3:49 PM EST
Moon enters Taurus ♉ 9:27 PM EST

*Potato & Onion Health & Magic*

# August 2020

**MONDAY, AUGUST 10**

**TUESDAY, AUGUST 11**
 Last Quarter 12:44 PM EST

**WEDNESDAY, AUGUST 12**
▶ Moon void-of-course begins 3:54 AM EST
Moon enters Gemini Ⅱ 9:45 AM EST

**THURSDAY, AUGUST 13**

**FRIDAY, AUGUST 14**
▶ Moon void-of-course begins 7:19 AM EST
Moon enters Cancer ♋ 7:35 PM EST

**SATURDAY, AUGUST 15**
♅ ℞ Uranus Retrograde 7:04 AM - Jan. 14, 2021

**SUNDAY, AUGUST 16**
▶ Moon void-of-course begins 7:58 PM EST

Rye - Love

Barley
Good Health

Beer - The Cycle of Life and Death

Witch's
BREW

# August 2020

## MONDAY, AUGUST 17
Moon enters Leo ♌ 1:38 AM EST

## TUESDAY, AUGUST 18
● New Moon 10:41 PM EST

## WEDNESDAY, AUGUST 19
▶ Moon void-of-course begins 1:38 AM EST
Moon enters Virgo ♍ 4:20 AM EST

## THURSDAY, AUGUST 20
▶ Moon void-of-course begins 11:36 PM EST

## FRIDAY, AUGUST 21
Moon enters Libra ♎ 5:15 AM EST

## SATURDAY, AUGUST 22
✿ Sun enters Virgo ♍

## SUNDAY, AUGUST 23
▶ Moon void-of-course begins 12:19 AM EST
Moon enters Scorpio ♏ 6:15 AM EST

Honeydew - Orange - Fig

Happiness

Blackberry - Basil - Lemon

Energy

Peach - Nectarine - Cinnamon

Love

# August 2020

## MONDAY, AUGUST 24

## TUESDAY, AUGUST 25
▶ Moon void-of-course begins 2:27 AM EST
Moon enters Sagittarius ♐ 8:48 AM EST
◑ First Quarter 1:57 PM EST

## WEDNESDAY, AUGUST 26

## THURSDAY, AUGUST 27
▶ Moon void-of-course begins 7:59 AM EST
Moon enters Capricorn ♑ 1:36 PM EST

## FRIDAY, AUGUST 28

## SATURDAY, AUGUST 29
▶ Moon void-of-course begins 3:30 PM EST
Moon enters Aquarius ♒ 8:36 PM EST

## SUNDAY, AUGUST 30

*Matcha - Cream - Blueberry*

*Strength & Protection*

*Black Tea - Plum - Ginger*

*Adventure*

# August/September 2020

## MONDAY, AUGUST 31

## TUESDAY, SEPTEMBER 1
▶ Moon void-of-course begins 12:56 AM EST
Moon enters Pisces ♓ 5:34 AM EST

## WEDNESDAY, SEPTEMBER 2
◯ Full Moon 1:21 AM EST

## THURSDAY, SEPTEMBER 3
▶ Moon void-of-course begins 10:34 AM EST
Moon enters Aries ♈ 4:21 PM EST

## FRIDAY, SEPTEMBER 4

## SATURDAY, SEPTEMBER 5

## SUNDAY, SEPTEMBER 6
▶ Moon void-of-course begins 12:44 AM EST
Moon enters Taurus ♉ 4:43 AM EST

*Sunflower Happiness*

Amber - Mental Clarity

"KING PUCK"
Mountain Goat
Strength & Endurance

# INTUITION:

_____

_____

_____

_____

_____

# REFLECTION:

_____

_____

_____

_____

_____

# VISION & INTENTION:

_____

_____

_____

_____

# IMPORTANT THINGS:

_____

_____

_____

_____

# GOALS:

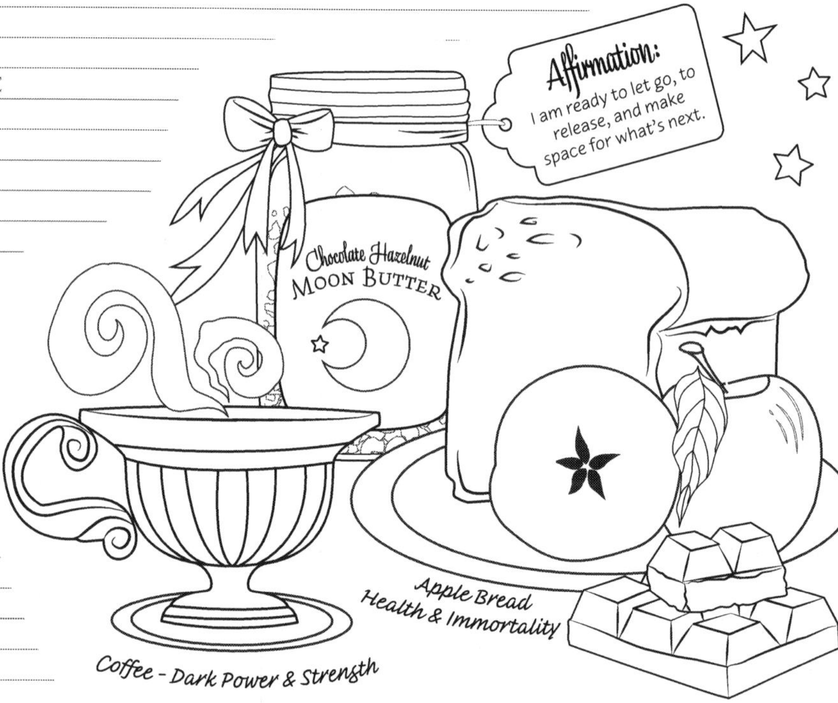

**Affirmation:**
I am ready to let go, to release, and make space for what's next.

*Chocolate Hazelnut*
MOON BUTTER

*Apple Bread*
*Health & Immortality*

*Coffee - Dark Power & Strength*

# September

*Chrysanthemum - Protection*

*Sage - Cleansing & Spirituality*

*Amethyst - Spiritual Awareness*

# Harvest Moon

## MOON ENERGY AND SPELL IDEAS

NEW & WAXING MOON: Accepting loss. Recovering from grief. Preparing for change.
FULL MOON: Assessment and balance. Finding courage to make change, transform, or let go.
WANING & DARK MOON: Releasing bitterness, attachment, and things that no longer serve you.

Labradorite
Raising Consciousness

Pour white wine in a silver cup
and gaze at the moon's reflection

# SCRYING WITH WATER
## ELEMENTAL WISDOM FROM THE DEPTHS OF EMOTION

*If you need more information, read the **Scrying & Divination Basics** in the intro of this book.*

Autumn is the season associated with water, emotions, evening, clearing away what's been harvested, and releasing or letting go of what is no longer needed.

Scrying with water, also called hydromancy, is a soothing and mystical form of divination. The "classic" method is to gaze at the surface of a still, reflective body of water. It could be a natural body of water such as a lake, pond, or puddle, or, you can fill a vessel with spring water —silver, brass, or a dark color like black will work best. You can also gaze at running water, such as a waterfall or stream.

The moon, a symbol of water, is often used along with this element. Try glinting the moon's light off a vessel or a body of water and gazing at the reflection. Or look for shapes to form as the moon dances off waves or watery ripples.

You can also watch flowing water to see if any faces or symbols appear. Use a camera to snap photos and check them out later... you never know when elemental spirits might visit you in a photograph.

You could also ask a question, then submerge yourself in water... and listen. Of course, in this situation, whether in a bath or in a natural body of water, always use extreme caution, good judgment, and common sense while swimming and submerging yourself.

You can also use the realm of your mind to scry with water in other dimensions—such as a faerie scrying pool or a mermaid grotto.

*Pears – Love & Magic*

# Mabon

*Toffee & Molasses*
*Divination & Magical Power*

*Nuts*
*Survival & Preparedness*

## RECIPROCITY RITUAL
### GIVE-AND-TAKE FOR THE AUTUMNAL EQUINOX

The Autumnal Equinox, also known as Mabon, is one of two points of the year where day and night are equal—the balance of light and dark.

Many believe that for magic to manifest, you must reciprocate or give back in some way.

Mabon provides a natural time to reflect on your exchange of energy. It's also a potent day to make shifts, cuts, or rebalance what feels "off."

You'll need: Wine or tea. Bulbs to bury or indoor herbs to plant (optional).

WHAT SHALL YOU REAP? Have an honest look at your life. Do you feel stuck? Have you outgrown parts of your life? Think about what you need to cut or change through the perspective of harvesting.

When you harvest, the food gives you sustenance, then transforms into your life's next expression. Do the same for big changes — take them in, be grateful for the lessons, and accept the transformations.

WHAT SHALL YE SOW? What are you planting to give back? You might empower others or make beautiful things. Perhaps you volunteer or grow things in your garden. This is a unique proposition between yourself and divine spirit, and it may be more mundane than you think.

THE RITUAL: Set up an altar that represents balance within yourself. Burn yerba santa, rue, or sandalwood to help clear your emotions.

To signify what you are reaping, toast (with wine or tea) to the life and death of anything that you are letting go of.

To dedicate to what you will sow, plant bulbs or herbs that represent what you'll give back.

# September 2020

| | SUNDAY | MONDAY | TUESDAY |
|---|---|---|---|
| | 30 | 31 | 1 |
| | 6 | 7 | 8 |
| | 13 | 14 | 15 |
| | 20 | 21 | 22 ☆ MABON |
| | 27 | 28 | 29 |

| WEDNESDAY | THURSDAY | FRIDAY | SATURDAY |
|---|---|---|---|
| 2 ○ Full Moon | 3 | 4 | 5 |
| 9 | 10 ◑ Last Quarter | 11 | 12 |
| 16 | 17 ● New Moon | 18 | 19 |
| 23 ◐ First Quarter | 24 | 25 | 26 |
| 30 | 1 ○ Full Moon | 2 | 3 |

# September 2020

**MONDAY, SEPTEMBER 7**

**TUESDAY, SEPTEMBER 8**
▶ Moon void-of-course begins 8:46 AM EST
Moon enters Gemini ♊ 5:27 PM EST

**WEDNESDAY, SEPTEMBER 9**
♂℞ Mars Retrograde 6:08 PM - Nov. 13, 2020

**THURSDAY, SEPTEMBER 10**
◗ Last Quarter 5:25 AM EST

**FRIDAY, SEPTEMBER 11**
▶ Moon void-of-course begins 12:47 AM EST
Moon enters Cancer ♋ 4:22 AM EST

**SATURDAY, SEPTEMBER 12**
♃ Jupiter goes Direct 7:21 PM

**SUNDAY, SEPTEMBER 13**
▶ Moon void-of-course begins 8:04 AM EST
Moon enters Leo ♌ 11:32 AM EST

## GOBLIN MARKET
by Christina Rossetti (1862)

*Mornings and evenings*
*Maids heard the goblins cry:*
*"Come buy our orchard fruits,*
*Come buy, come buy:*
*Apples and quinces,*
*Lemons and oranges,*
*Plump unpecked cherries,*
*Melons and raspberries,*
*Bloom-down-cheeked peaches,*
*Swart-headed mulberries,*
*Wild free-born cranberries,*
*Crab-apples, dewberries,*
*Pine-apples, blackberries,*
*Apricots, strawberries; -*
*All ripe together*
*In summer weather, -*
*Morns that pass by,*
*Fair eves that fly;*
*Come buy, come buy."*

- An excerpt -
© Public Domain

# September 2020

## MONDAY, SEPTEMBER 14

## TUESDAY, SEPTEMBER 15
▶ Moon void-of-course begins 11:09 AM EST
Moon enters Virgo ♍ 2:37 PM EST

## WEDNESDAY, SEPTEMBER 16

## THURSDAY, SEPTEMBER 17
● New Moon 7:00 AM EST
▶ Moon void-of-course begins 7:41 AM EST
Moon enters Libra ♎ 2:55 PM EST

## FRIDAY, SEPTEMBER 18

## SATURDAY, SEPTEMBER 19
▶ Moon void-of-course begins 10:28 AM EST
Moon enters Scorpio ♏ 2:32 PM EST

## SUNDAY, SEPTEMBER 20

# September 2020

## MONDAY, SEPTEMBER 21
▶ Moon void-of-course begins 2:12 PM EST
Moon enters Sagittarius ♐ 3:31 PM EST

## TUESDAY, SEPTEMBER 22
☆ **MABON** Autumnal Equinox 9:31 AM EST
☼ Sun enters Libra ♎

## WEDNESDAY, SEPTEMBER 23
▶ Moon void-of-course begins 1:31 PM EST
Moon enters Capricorn ♑ 7:16 PM EST
◗ First Quarter 9:54 PM EST

## THURSDAY, SEPTEMBER 24

## FRIDAY, SEPTEMBER 25
▶ Moon void-of-course begins 11:35 PM EST

## SATURDAY, SEPTEMBER 26
Moon enters Aquarius ♒ 2:07 AM EST

## SUNDAY, SEPTEMBER 27

Fork - Divination & Decisions

Spoon - Directing Energy

Knife - Banishing & Releasing

# September/October 2020

## MONDAY, SEPTEMBER 28
▶ Moon void-of-course begins 3:17 AM EST
Moon enters Pisces ♓ 11:33 AM EST
♄ Saturn goes Direct 11:46 PM

## TUESDAY, SEPTEMBER 29

## WEDNESDAY, SEPTEMBER 30
▶ Moon void-of-course begins 1:29 PM EST
Moon enters Aries ♈ 10:46 PM EST

## THURSDAY, OCTOBER 1
○ Full Moon 5:05 PM EST

## FRIDAY, OCTOBER 2

## SATURDAY, OCTOBER 3
▶ Moon void-of-course begins 1:47 AM EST
Moon enters Taurus ♉ 11:12 AM EST

## SUNDAY, OCTOBER 4
♀ Pluto goes Direct 3:14 AM

*Broom - Magical Power & Freedom*
*Cauldron - Creation & Empowerment*

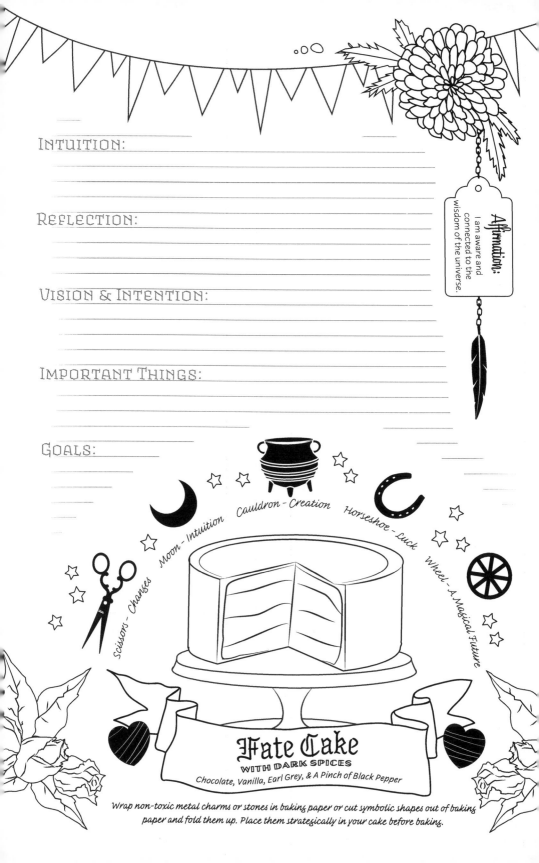

INTUITION:

REFLECTION:

VISION & INTENTION:

IMPORTANT THINGS:

GOALS:

Affirmation:
I am aware and connected to the wisdom of the universe.

Scissors - Changes
Moon - Intuition
Cauldron - Creation
Horseshoe - Luck
Wheel - A Magical Future

Fate Cake
WITH DARK SPICES
Chocolate, Vanilla, Earl Grey, & A Pinch of Black Pepper

Wrap non-toxic metal charms or stones in baking paper or cut symbolic shapes out of baking paper and fold them up. Place them strategically in your cake before baking.

# October

Marigold – Divination

Black Tourmaline – Banishing

Black Cats & Pumpkins – Magic

# Hunter's Moon

## MOON ENERGY AND SPELL IDEAS

NEW & WAXING MOON: Learning and healing from the past. Increasing psychic awareness.
FULL MOON: Transformation and divining messages from ancestors and spirit guides.
WANING & DARK MOON: Release from old emotional patterns, beliefs, and attachments.

Affirmation:
I am full of magic. Wondrous things await me.

Have Some Tea
So Mote It Be

Blueberry Cheesecake
Happiness

Apatite
Spiritual Inspiration

Sodalite
Enlightened State of Mind

Unicorn - The Unexpected

Blue Pea Flower Tea - Love

Blue Chrysanthemum - Tranquility

# BLUE MOON

## MOON ENERGY AND SPELL IDEAS

NEW & WAXING MOON: Growing your power and strength. Making things happen.
FULL MOON: Calling in that which is delightfully unexpected. Massive transformations.
WANING & DARK MOON: Deep silence and connection to intuitive guidance.

LIGHT

SHADOW

Black Dog
Protection & the Shadow-Self

# THE KEYS TO THE CROSSROADS
## FINDING WISDOM IN THE DARK

As Samhain approaches, the seasonal shift is marked as the color drains from leaves, and the Wheel turns towards darkness.

Hecate is a Greek goddess of magic, the underworld, and the moon. She's revered in modern day as a "dark" goddess, which doesn't mean "evil," but signifies the magic found in using the wisdom of the dark and the unknown to empower yourself as opposed to fearing the dark. Hecate is often pictured holding the keys to the crossroads of the earthly plane and the spiritual realms.

Whether or not you work with Hecate, you can enchant a key to unlock the wisdom of the depths of yourself. A lock and key represent how we are our own enemies: the lock, our own limits—and the key—that we ultimately have the power to unclasp the bindings.

THINGS YOU'LL NEED: A key—any kind—old or new. Consecrate and clear the energy of the key if it's been used. You may want to take extra precautions and bury it in a pot of earth for a moon cycle if you don't know the origins of it. Craft a keychain with beads, ribbon, shells, crystals, charms, or what feels powerful.

CAST THE SPELL: Run your key through a flame or the smoke of a dark incense such as frankincense, juniper berries, and sandalwood.

Charm your key by chanting the following:

*Three times three, when I turn this key,*
*I'll learn the secrets of the crossroads*
*In the shadows cast by me.*

Turn the key nine times in your hand or pocket anytime you require wisdom of the dark.

## Wisdom
What wisdom can I learn from my ancestral past?

## Quest
What challenge from our lineage must I rise to meet?

## Vision
What can the ancestors see that I cannot yet see?

# Ancestral Tarot

# Samhain

## SAMHAIN SÉANCE

### A RITUAL CALL TO LOVED ONES IN THE SPIRIT WORLD

The experience of witnessing the ancestral presence in a séance is one of wholeness, belonging, and deep acceptance of yourself in the larger scheme of life.

To prepare for a séance, think about who you will call. It's advisable to contact those that knew and loved you. Procure their picture or a representation of them. If you don't have a specific spirit to call, you can contact "the benevolent ancestral spirits that came before."

Choose a way to communicate such as tarot cards, runes, or a spirit board. You don't need any tools if you can listen very closely, however, divination tools are powerful and useful.

Light candles, as spirits are attracted to the warmth and light. Burn incense to raise the spiritual energy as well as protect the space, such as a mixture of frankincense and sandalwood. You may like to drink a spiritually elevating tea such as wormwood or a blend of mugwort, yarrow, and lavender.

Cast a circle and set a strong protective spell of white or gold light. Say a few words to honor the benevolent spirits of those that loved you. Then, invite them to join at their own free will. Take a few moments of silence or energy raising. Humming, chanting, or singing are all super powerful energy techniques.

When you feel the presence of the spirits, begin asking questions aloud, just like a conversation. Use your divination tools or listen closely to your feelings and intuition.

When you are done, make sure to close your circle and "close the door" to the spirit world.

# October 2020

| SUNDAY | MONDAY | TUESDAY |
|--------|--------|---------|
| 27 | 28 | 29 |
| 4 | 5 | 6 |
| 11 | 12 | 13 |
| 18 | 19 | 20 |
| 25 | 26 | 27 |

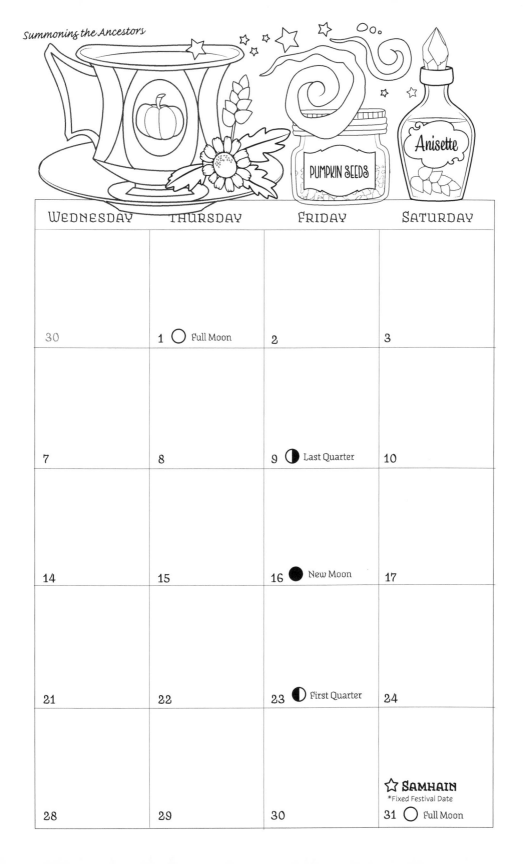

Summoning the Ancestors

| WEDNESDAY | THURSDAY | FRIDAY | SATURDAY |
|---|---|---|---|
| 30 | 1 ◯ Full Moon | 2 | 3 |
| 7 | 8 | 9 ◐ Last Quarter | 10 |
| 14 | 15 | 16 ● New Moon | 17 |
| 21 | 22 | 23 ◑ First Quarter | 24 |
| 28 | 29 | 30 | ☆ **SAMHAIN** <br> *Fixed Festival Date <br> 31 ◯ Full Moon |

# October 2020

## MONDAY, OCTOBER 5
▶ Moon void-of-course begins 2:40 PM EST

## TUESDAY, OCTOBER 6
Moon enters Gemini Ⅱ 12:02 AM EST

## WEDNESDAY, OCTOBER 7
▶ Moon void-of-course begins 9:56 PM EST

## THURSDAY, OCTOBER 8
Moon enters Cancer ♋ 11:45 AM EST

## FRIDAY, OCTOBER 9
◐ Last Quarter 8:39 PM EST

## SATURDAY, OCTOBER 10
▶ Moon void-of-course begins 12:03 PM EST
Moon enters Leo ♌ 8:24 PM EST

## SUNDAY, OCTOBER 11

*Aconite (Wolfsbane)*
*Protection*

# October 2020

### MONDAY, OCTOBER 12
▶ Moon void-of-course begins 10:29 AM EST

### TUESDAY, OCTOBER 13
Moon enters Virgo ♍ 12:55 AM EST
☿℞ Mercury Retrograde 8:58 PM - Nov. 3, 2020

### WEDNESDAY, OCTOBER 14
▶ Moon void-of-course begins 6:46 PM EST

### THURSDAY, OCTOBER 15
Moon enters Libra ♎ 1:53 AM EST

### FRIDAY, OCTOBER 16
● New Moon 3:30 PM EST
▶ Moon void-of-course begins 6:11 PM EST

### SATURDAY, OCTOBER 17
Moon enters Scorpio ♏ 1:05 AM EST

### SUNDAY, OCTOBER 18
▶ Moon void-of-course begins 5:42 PM EST

# October 2020

*Scarecrow
Energetic Protection*

## MONDAY, OCTOBER 19
Moon enters Sagittarius ♐ 12:42 AM EST

## TUESDAY, OCTOBER 20
▶ Moon void-of-course begins 11:37 PM EST

## WEDNESDAY, OCTOBER 21
Moon enters Capricorn ♑ 2:43 PM EST

## THURSDAY, OCTOBER 22
✿ Sun enters Scorpio

## FRIDAY, OCTOBER 23
▶ Moon void-of-course begins 12:34 AM EST
Moon enters Aquarius ♒ 8:16 AM EST
◑ First Quarter 9:22 AM EST

## SATURDAY, OCTOBER 24
▶ Moon void-of-course begins 5:53 PM EST

## SUNDAY, OCTOBER 25
Moon enters Pisces ♓ 5:18 PM EST

*Fill a charm bag with protective stones and herbs such as jet, roots, and rosemary. Place it inside your scarecrow for extra power.*

# October/November 2020

## MONDAY, OCTOBER 26

*Spiders*
*Creation, Binding, & Banishing*

## TUESDAY, OCTOBER 27

▶ Moon void-of-course begins 8:45 PM EST

## WEDNESDAY, OCTOBER 28

Moon enters Aries ♈ 4:44 AM EST

*Samhain Chant\**

*"Dance the ring, luck to bring,*
*When the year's aturning,*
*Chant the rhyme at Hallowstime,*
*When the fire's burning."*
*- Doreen Valiente*
*"WitchCraft for Tomorrow"*

## THURSDAY, OCTOBER 29

## FRIDAY, OCTOBER 30

▶ Moon void-of-course begins 12:12 PM EST
Moon enters Taurus ♉ 5:18 PM EST

## SATURDAY, OCTOBER 31

☆ **Samhain**
\*Fixed Festival Date
◯ Full Moon 10:49 AM EST

## SUNDAY, NOVEMBER 1

▶ Moon void-of-course begins 9:29 PM EST

\*Published with permission.
*WitchCraft for Tomorrow* by Doreen Valiente
© The Crowood Press Ltd. ISBN 978-0709052449

INTUITION:

REFLECTION:

VISION & INTENTION:

IMPORTANT THINGS:

GOALS:

Mugwort & Black Tea
with Rose Hips

Affirmation:
I am a cosmic being.

Psychic Powers

# NOVEMBER

Onyx – Inner Power

Alyssum – Protection & Peaceful Energy

Cosmos – Love & Beauty

Bats – Subconscious & Otherworldly Messages

# SNOW MOON

## MOON ENERGY AND SPELL IDEAS

NEW & WAXING MOON: Increasing coziness, comfort at home, and the simple joys of life.
FULL MOON: Interconnectedness and spiritual transcendence. Connection with others.
WANING & DARK MOON: Inward reflection. Releasing sorrow and feelings of isolation.

Shunsite
Spiritual Evolution

Nebula Stone - Spiritual Depth

# Ritual of the Unknown
## A Spell That Unfolds Before You

When all else fails or you don't know what to do... do this Ritual of the Unknown!

Often, the magic is in the mysterious. And this spell (or ritual) will allow the message, intention, and magic to unfold before you, even if you have no idea what your spell will be about.

You'll need: nothing other than gratitude for what's unfolded in your life so far. You can prepare a spell candle, incense, meditative music, or other embellishments if desired.

Cast your circle and perform any opening ceremonies that you like. Chant repeatedly until you are in a meditative state, or just take a few moments to meditate. Use a chant like the one below, or any of your choosing.

*As I face the dark unknown,*
*Let the magic of this spell be shown.*

Then, just speak from your heart, straight to your divine. You might not need to speak anything, as a feeling or energy may come to you. You can ask a question or just sit in reverence.

Then, let the magic unfold! Clear your mind and wait for a message. It can be a thought, a feeling, or a sense of knowing. If you prefer to "do something, " try writing in a journal until you find that spark of intuitive thought or use tarot cards or another form of divination to help you connect.

Once the message has come forward, reflect on it for a few moments and take it to heart. Then thank the divine source or deity and close your circle. Make sure to write down anything you experience, feel, or learn.

# November 2020

| SUNDAY | MONDAY | TUESDAY |
|--------|--------|---------|
| 1 | 2 | 3 |
| 8 ◐ Last Quarter | 9 | 10 |
| 15 ● New Moon | 16 | 17 |
| 22 | 23 | 24 |
| 29 | 30 ○ Full Moon | 1 |

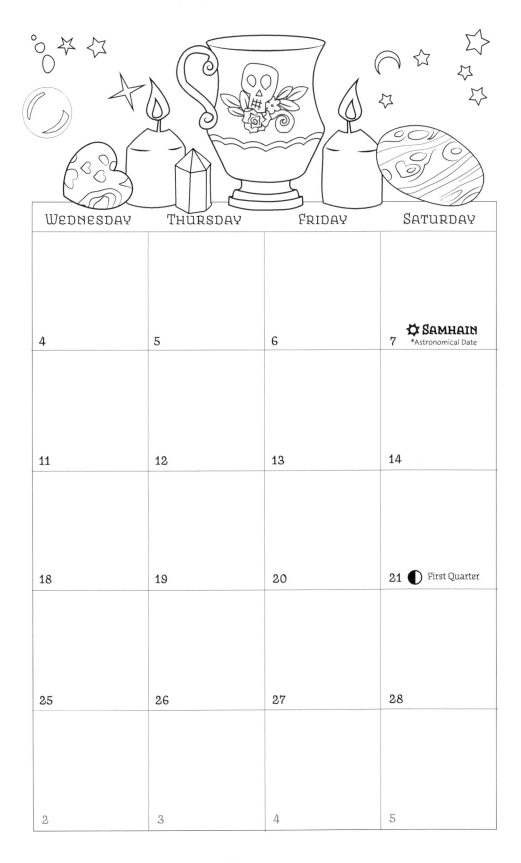

| WEDNESDAY | THURSDAY | FRIDAY | SATURDAY |
|---|---|---|---|
| 4 | 5 | 6 | 7 ☼ **SAMHAIN** *Astronomical Date |
| 11 | 12 | 13 | 14 |
| 18 | 19 | 20 | 21 ◗ First Quarter |
| 25 | 26 | 27 | 28 |
| 2 | 3 | 4 | 5 |

# November 2020

### MONDAY, NOVEMBER 2
Moon enters Gemini ♊ 4:59 AM EST

*Carry a green flannel charm bag filled with dill to bring wealth & abundance*

### TUESDAY, NOVEMBER 3
☿ Mercury goes Direct 12:44 PM

### WEDNESDAY, NOVEMBER 4
▶ Moon void-of-course begins 8:48 AM EST
Moon enters Cancer ♋ 4:45 PM EST

### THURSDAY, NOVEMBER 5

### FRIDAY, NOVEMBER 6
▶ Moon void-of-course begins 8:26 PM EST

### SATURDAY, NOVEMBER 7
Moon enters Leo ♌ 2:18 AM EST
☼ **Samhain** 5:56 PM EST
*Astronomical Date

### SUNDAY, NOVEMBER 8
◐ Last Quarter 8:45 AM EST

*Handbag – Hidden Power & Prosperity*

# November 2020

### MONDAY, NOVEMBER 9
▶ Moon void-of-course begins 6:04 AM EST
Moon enters Virgo ♍ 8:29 AM EST

### TUESDAY, NOVEMBER 10

### WEDNESDAY, NOVEMBER 11
▶ Moon void-of-course begins 5:58 AM EST
Moon enters Libra ♎ 11:09 AM EST

### THURSDAY, NOVEMBER 12

### FRIDAY, NOVEMBER 13
▶ Moon void-of-course begins 6:32 AM EST
Moon enters Scorpio ♏ 11:18 AM EST
♂ Mars goes Direct 6:48 PM

### SATURDAY, NOVEMBER 14

### SUNDAY, NOVEMBER 15
● New Moon 12:07 AM EST
▶ Moon void-of-course begins 6:12 AM EST
Moon enters Sagittarius ♐ 10:46 AM EST

*Umbrella - protection*

# November 2020

## MONDAY, NOVEMBER 16

## TUESDAY, NOVEMBER 17
▶ Moon void-of-course begins 2:54 AM EST
Moon enters Capricorn ♑ 11:34 AM EST

## WEDNESDAY, NOVEMBER 18

## THURSDAY, NOVEMBER 19
▶ Moon void-of-course begins 11:29 AM EST
Moon enters Aquarius ♒ 3:24 PM EST

## FRIDAY, NOVEMBER 20
▶ Moon void-of-course begins 7:48 PM EST

## SATURDAY, NOVEMBER 21
✿ Sun enters Sagittarius ♐
Moon enters Pisces ♓ 11:05 PM EST
◗ First Quarter 11:44 PM EST

## SUNDAY, NOVEMBER 22

*If the Shoes Fit...*
*Get a Broom and*
*Hat to Match.*

*Rub one drop of cedar or musk oil*
*in each shoe to increase your courage.*

# November 2020

## MONDAY, NOVEMBER 23

## TUESDAY, NOVEMBER 24
▶ Moon void-of-course begins 5:44 AM EST
Moon enters Aries ♈ 10:04 AM EST

## WEDNESDAY, NOVEMBER 25

## THURSDAY, NOVEMBER 26
▶ Moon void-of-course begins 6:45 PM EST
Moon enters Taurus ♉ 10:42 PM EST

## FRIDAY, NOVEMBER 27

## SATURDAY, NOVEMBER 28
♆ Neptune goes Direct 7:36 PM

## SUNDAY, NOVEMBER 29
▶ Moon void-of-course begins 7:48 AM EST
Moon enters Gemini ♊ 11:15 AM EST

# November/December 20

**MONDAY, NOVEMBER 30**
○ Full Moon 4:29 AM EST
▶ Moon void-of-course begins 11:21 PM EST

**TUESDAY, DECEMBER 1**
Moon enters Cancer ♋ 10:32 PM EST

**WEDNESDAY, DECEMBER 2**

**THURSDAY, DECEMBER 3**

**FRIDAY, DECEMBER 4**
▶ Moon void-of-course begins 5:28 AM EST
Moon enters Leo ♌ 7:52 AM EST

**SATURDAY, DECEMBER 5**
▶ Moon void-of-course begins 5:27 PM EST

ABRACADABRA
BRACADABRA
RACADABRA
CADABRA
ADABRA
DABRA
ABRA
BRA
RA
A

**SUNDAY, DECEMBER 6**
Moon enters Virgo ♍ 2:46 PM EST

*Book of Shadows – Personal Expression & Empowerment*
*Pen & Pencil – The Power of Creation & Storytelling*

# Abracadabra
Ancient Words of Power

A spell to release or diminish something:
Write the full word, "ABRACADABRA." On the next line, repeat the word but omit the first letter. Omit one additional letter on each line until you end with just the last "A."

A spell to heal or create something:
Start by writing just the first letter "A." Add one additional letter to the word on each line until you end with the full word, ABRACADABRA.

INTUITION:

_____
_____
_____
_____
_____
_____

REFLECTION:

_____
_____
_____
_____
_____

VISION & INTENTION:

_____
_____
_____
_____
_____

IMPORTANT THINGS:

_____
_____
_____
_____

**Affirmation:**
I rest, relax, and sit in
peace with the unknown.

GOALS:

_____
_____
_____
_____

Amaryllis
Devotion & Love

Stitch
Witch

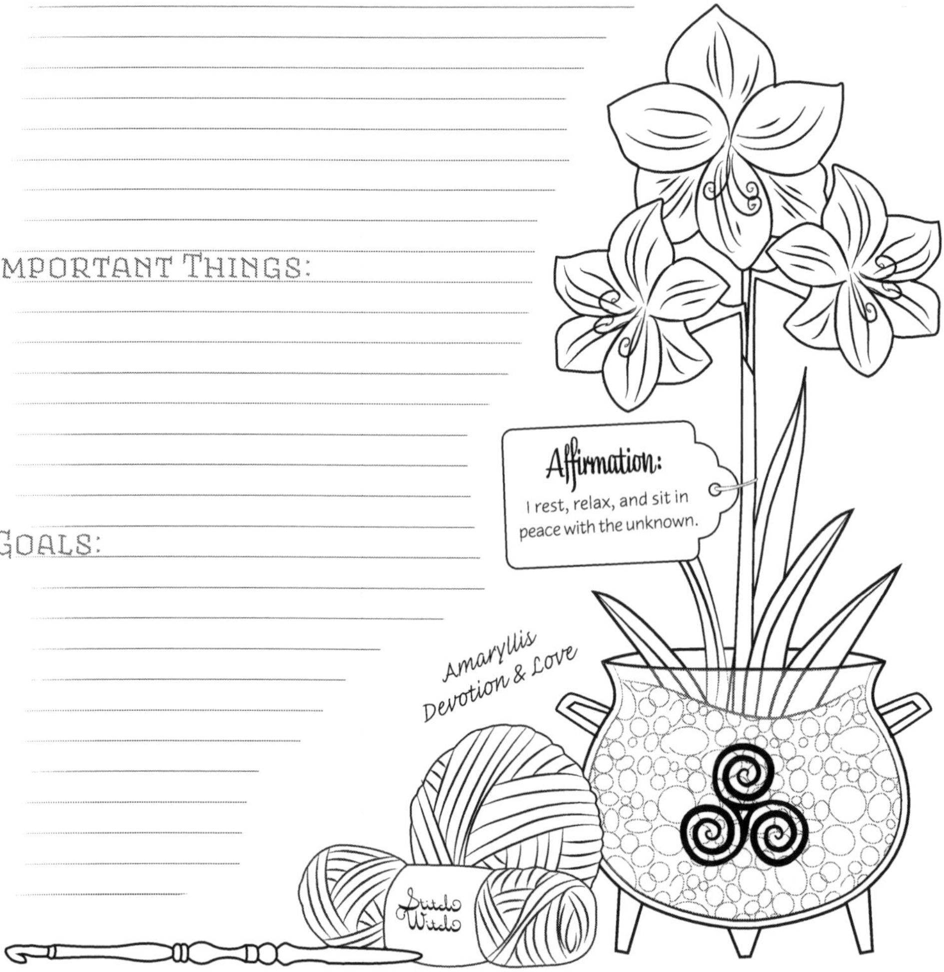

# DECEMBER

Serpentine - Groundings & Spiritual Growth

Rose Hip Branches - Serenity & Peace

Paperwhite Narcissus - Purity & Beauty

# OAK MOON

## MOON ENERGY AND SPELL IDEAS

NEW & WAXING MOON: Increasing rest and relaxation. Enhancing a jolly mood and spirit.
FULL MOON: Rebirth and transformation. Recognizing your brilliance and light.
WANING & DARK MOON: Releasing to the universe. Respite and surrender to the unknown.

Jet - Protection & Spiritual Evolution

Rose Quartz - Love

Gold Sheen Obsidian
Unearthing Hidden Knowledge

Black Jasper
Deep Visions

Christmas Cactus
Hope Amidst Darkness

Clear Quartz - Channeling Energy

Labradorite - Raising Consciousness

Apophyllite Pyramid
Opening the Third Eye

# SCRYING WITH EARTH
## THE GROUNDING WISDOM OF STONES AND BONES

As the seasons shift to winter and the element of earth, what do you feel in the depths of your soul? Make sure to use any quiet opportunities that arise to slip away and look for wondrous messages to appear from your intuition.

MIRRORS, STONES, & CRYSTAL BALLS

Scrying mirrors are often made of stones like obsidian, which have a black mirror-like finish when polished. They can also be made of glass painted black, of polished metal such as silver or brass, or of anything reflective, like a crystal ball.

When scrying into a mirror or ball, gaze at it from an angle so you don't see your reflection. If it's a clear crystal, gaze into the depths. If it's an opaque stone, gaze at the surface. Experiment with using a candle behind or in front of your scrying tool, or by wafting herbal smoke for both magical and visual enhancement.

You can also scry with a "regular" mirror and candle in a pitch-dark room. Place the candle between yourself and the mirror. Gaze your eyes about eighteen inches away from the mirror, take your time, and look for extraordinary messages to appear in the smoke, in the reflections, and in your consciousness.

RUNE STONES tap into the element of earth as they are commonly made of stones or circles of wood. Rune stones are often cast onto a cloth and the positions and symbols are divined therein.

THROWING BONES are an otherworldly form of earth divination. The symbolism of the bone sets and techniques used are personal and varied.

And, you can listen literally to the earth. Put your ear to the ground and see what you hear.

# Yule

Magic cookies filled with ginger,
Light me up this dark of winter
Wish I may, I wish I might,
Bewitch myself this solstice night.

*Allspice*

*Ginger*
*Attraction & Power*

*NUTMEG*

*Cloves*

*Cinnamon*
*Divine Energy*

# GINGERBREAD COOKIE SPELL
## KITCHEN WITCHERY TO ATTRACT WHAT YOU DESIRE

Gingerbread is delicious and has been used in spellwork for hundreds of years. Its powers of attraction were commonly known in medieval Europe, where women ate gingerbread men to bewitch themselves and attract a (spicy yet sweet!) husband. And you've likely heard of the witch's gingerbread house in *Hansel and Gretel*.

Gingerbread is alluring. When you consider the herbs and spices used in gingerbread, it's no wonder it has such a magnificent quality of attraction. Molasses and ginger are filled with power. Cinnamon brings in connection to divine energy. Allspice and nutmeg will uplift your spirits and vibration. And cloves are a powerful symbol of love and richness of life.

And so, witch up your gingerbread this Yule to attract whatever you desire.

THINGS YOU'LL NEED: Prepare to make gingerbread cookies, including all of the spices above. Use fresh ginger if possible, and consider doubling the amount of spice in your recipe.

PERFORM THE SPELL: Mix up your dough on the solstice. Roll it out and cut it into the shape of what you desire. Use cookie cutters or just a knife. Bake according to your recipe. Decorate using sprinkles and icing of symbolic colors.

State the intention of what you wish. Then repeat the chant above three times while clapping rhythmically at an increasing speed.

Then eat a cookie! Close your eyes. Feel the warmth of the spice drawing in the energy of what you want to attract. Continue to feel good for as many days as you can. Repeat as you are called, until all of the cookies are gone.

# December 2020

| Sunday | Monday | Tuesday |
|---|---|---|
| 29 | 30 ◯ Full Moon | 1 |
| 6 | 7 ◑ Last Quarter | 8 |
| 13 | 14 ● New Moon | 15 |
| 20 | ☆ Yule<br>21 ◑ First Quarter | 22 |
| 27 | 28 | 29 ◯ Full Moon |

| WEDNESDAY | THURSDAY | FRIDAY | SATURDAY |
|-----------|----------|--------|----------|
| 2 | 3 | 4 | 5 |
| 9 | 10 | 11 | 12 |
| 16 | 17 | 18 | 19 |
| 23 | 24 | 25 | 26 |
| 30 | 31 | 1 | 2 |

# December 2020

*Revitalization & Healing*
*Eucalyptus - Bergamot - Lemon*

## MONDAY, DECEMBER 7

◑ Last Quarter 7:36 PM EST

## TUESDAY, DECEMBER 8

▶ Moon void-of-course begins 5:35 PM EST
Moon enters Libra ♎ 7:01 PM EST

## WEDNESDAY, DECEMBER 9

## THURSDAY, DECEMBER 10

▶ Moon void-of-course begins 7:56 PM EST
Moon enters Scorpio ♏ 8:57 PM EST

## FRIDAY, DECEMBER 11

New Moon
Ritual Bath

*Magical Black Soap*
*Activated Charcoal - Calendula - Rose Petals*
*Chamomile - Tea Tree Oil - Rosemary - Sage*

## SATURDAY, DECEMBER 12

▶ Moon void-of-course begins 8:57 PM EST
Moon enters Sagittarius ♐ 9:39 PM EST

## SUNDAY, DECEMBER 13

*Sweet Dreams*
*Coco Butter - Vanilla - Cinnamon - Sandalwood*

# December 2020

## MONDAY, DECEMBER 14
● New Moon 11:16 AM EST
▶ Moon void-of-course begins 11:16 AM EST
Moon enters Capricorn ♑ 10:34 PM EST

## TUESDAY, DECEMBER 15

## WEDNESDAY, DECEMBER 16

## THURSDAY, DECEMBER 17
▶ Moon void-of-course begins 12:34 AM EST
Moon enters Aquarius ♒ 1:26 AM EST

## FRIDAY, DECEMBER 18

## SATURDAY, DECEMBER 19
▶ Moon void-of-course begins 3:44 AM EST
Moon enters Pisces ♓ 7:38 AM EST

## SUNDAY, DECEMBER 20

to: Fiona

Phyllis

Starhawk

# December 2020

## MONDAY, DECEMBER 21

☆ **Yule – Winter Solstice** 5:02 AM EST
✿ Sun enters Capricorn ♑
▶ Moon void-of-course begins 5:24 AM EST
Moon enters Aries ♈ 5:32 PM EST
◑ First Quarter 6:41 PM EST

## TUESDAY, DECEMBER 22

## WEDNESDAY, DECEMBER 23
▶ Moon void-of-course begins 5:50 PM EST

## THURSDAY, DECEMBER 24
Moon enters Taurus ♉ 5:55 AM EST

## FRIDAY, DECEMBER 25

## SATURDAY, DECEMBER 26
▶ Moon void-of-course begins 6:31 AM EST
Moon enters Gemini ♊ 6:32 PM EST

## SUNDAY, DECEMBER 27

Winter Solstice
INCENSE

Red Myrrh
Cedar
Sandalwood
Dragon's Blood
Frankincense
Juniper Berries

# December 2020/ January 2021

## MONDAY, DECEMBER 28
▶ Moon void-of-course begins 8:00 PM EST

## TUESDAY, DECEMBER 29
Moon enters Cancer ♋ 5:28 AM EST
○ Full Moon 10:28 PM EST

## WEDNESDAY, DECEMBER 30

## THURSDAY, DECEMBER 31
▶ Moon void-of-course begins 8:44 AM EST
Moon enters Leo ♌ 1:58 PM EST

## FRIDAY, JANUARY 1, 2021

## SATURDAY, JANUARY 2, 2021
▶ Moon void-of-course begins 4:59 PM EST
Moon enters Virgo ♍ 8:13 PM EST

## SUNDAY, JANUARY 3, 2021

WILL
LOGIC
HEART
HEAD
LIFE
LOVE
SUN
FATE
HEALTH

BRACELETS OF LIFE

# New Year's

**LESSONS**
What've I learned or overcome this year?

**SUCCESS**
What was my biggest success?

**GRATITUDE**
What am I most grateful for in this past year?

*Looking Back*

2020

**RELEASE**
What is best left behind?

**RECEIVE**
What was 2020's unexpected gift?

Ask these questions with any sort of divination tool such as tarot cards, oracle cards, or rune stones. You can also use them as journaling prompts without any divination tools.

# Tarot Spread

### Opportunity
Where does my greatest opportunity lie?

### Focus
Where should I focus my energy as the year begins?

### Challenge
What challenge lies ahead?

### Wisdom
What wisdom will guide me forward in the best way possible?

### Magic
What new skills, powers, or magic should I cultivate?

## Moving Forward
### 2021

# Bibliography & Special Thanks

*(in alphabetical order)*

A Kitchen Witch's Cookbook - Patricia Telesco
A Witch's Guide to Faery Folk - Edain McCoy
Autumn Equinox - Ellen Dugan
Candlemas - Amber K & Azrael Arynn K
Celtic Folklore Cooking - Joanne Asala
Celtic Lore & Spellcraft of the Dark Goddess -Stephanie Woodfield
Celtic Myth & Magic - Edain McCoy
Cunningham's Encyclopedia of Magical Herbs - Scott Cunningham
Dark Moon Magic - Cerridwen Greenleaf
Drawing the Light from Within - Dr. Judith Cornell
Encyclopedia of Spells - Judika Illes
Faery Wicca - Kisma K.Stephanich
Halloween - Silver Ravenwolf
Lammas: Celebrating the Fruits of the First Harvest - Franklin & Mason
Llewellyn's Little Book of Halloween - Mickie Mueller
Llewellyn's Sabbat Series (Various Authors)
Mandala - Dr. Judith Cornell
Midsummer - Anna Franklin
Ostara - Edain McCoy
Seasons of Witchery - Ellen Dugan
The Art of Witch - Fiona Horne
The Great Work - Tiffany Lazic
The Hedgewitch's Book of Days - Mandy Mitchell
The Kitchen Witch - Soraya
The Wheel of the Year - Pauline & Dan Campanelli
The Women's Dictionary of Symbols and Sacred Objects - Barbara Walker
WitchCraft for Tomorrow - Doreen Valiente
Yule: A Celebration of the Light Within - Dorothy Morrison

*Samhain Chant, pg. 151, is an excerpt from WitchCraft for Tomorrow by Doreen Valiente,
© The Crowood Press Ltd. ISBN 978-0709052449. Published here with permission. Thanks so much!*

**Wendy Ledger**
Editor
*WendyLedgerAuthor.com*

**Fiona Horne**
Editor of Magick
*FionaHorne.com*

# About the Artist

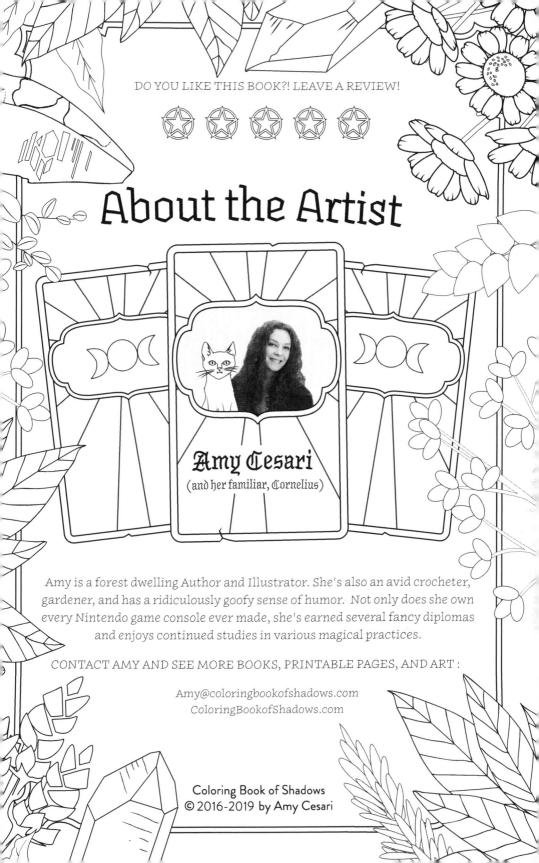

**Amy Cesari**
(and her familiar, Cornelius)

Amy is a forest dwelling Author and Illustrator. She's also an avid crocheter, gardener, and has a ridiculously goofy sense of humor. Not only does she own every Nintendo game console ever made, she's earned several fancy diplomas and enjoys continued studies in various magical practices.

CONTACT AMY AND SEE MORE BOOKS, PRINTABLE PAGES, AND ART :

Amy@coloringbookofshadows.com
ColoringBookofShadows.com

Brooms of Elder
Clearing the Energy of Your Life and Spirit

Made in the USA
Coppell, TX
29 December 2019